HOLDING JESUS

HOLDING
JESUS

Reflections ON MARY
THE MOTHER OF GOD

ALFRED MCBRIDE, O.PRAEM.

Franciscan
MEDIA
Cincinnati, Ohio

Unless otherwise indicated, Scripture passages have been taken from *New Revised Standard Version Bible,* copyright ©1989 by the Division of Christian Education of the National Council of the Churches of Christ in the U.S.A., and used by permission. All rights reserved. Quotes from the English translation of the *Catechism of the Catholic Church:* Modifications from the Editio Typica copyright © 1997, United States Catholic Conference, Inc. —Libreria Editrice Vaticana are used by permission.

Cover design by Candle Light Studios
Cover image © Annika Photography | Belgium
Book design by Mark Sullivan

LIBRARY OF CONGRESS CATALOGING-IN-PUBLICATION DATA
McBride, Alfred.
Holding Jesus : reflections on Mary, the Mother of God / Alfred McBride.
p. cm.
Includes bibliographical references and index.
ISBN 978-1-61636-480-9 (alk. paper)
1. Mary, Blessed Virgin, Saint—Meditations. 2. Advent—Meditations. 3. Christmas—Meditations. 4. Mary, Blessed Virgin, Saint—Coredemption. I. Title.
BT608.5.M374 2012
232.91—dc23
2012015048

Copyright © 2012, by Alfred McBride, O.PRAEM. All rights reserved.
ISBN 978-1-61636-480-9

Published by Franciscan Media
28 W. Liberty St.
Cincinnati, OH 45202
www.FranciscanMedia.org

Printed in the United States of America.
Printed on acid-free paper.
12 13 14 15 16   5 4 3 2 1

To Mary, the Mother of Jesus,
who has been a faithful mother figure to me
throughout my sixty years in the priesthood.
Her prayers and spiritual encouragement
have guided and carried me
through it all.

I offer her this book as a thank you
for holding me close to Jesus.
Ave Maria.

| • CONTENTS • |

In faith we love to think of Mary as our Blessed Mother.

Throughout the last two millennia, we have seen Mary depicted again and again holding the infant Jesus in her arms. The most popular image of Mary in paintings, icons, stained glass, and statuary is her role as the Madonna, the Mother of the Word made flesh. The imagination and genius of artists supply us with images of the maternal wonder, innocence, and affection that our faith discerns in this holy Mother of God.

But the story of Mary's relationship with Jesus goes beyond her nurturing him as a child. She will also accompany him throughout his life from childhood to the teen years, from young adulthood to his maturity, from his thirtieth year to his Passion and Death, from his Resurrection to his Ascension.

Through all these stages, Mary continues to hold her Son in her love and in her outstanding prayer and contemplation. As a young wife and new mother, she holds him as a baby in Bethlehem. As the Mother of sorrows, she holds him again when he is taken down from the cross. And then in the Upper Room at Pentecost, she extends her love by holding the mystical Body of Christ—the infant Church, made real by the descent of the Holy Spirit.

Holding Jesus approaches Mary's relationship with her Son in three parts:

- Part one provides a walk with Mary as mother of the child Jesus, with reflections for each day of Advent leading up to and concluding with Christmas. The Advent readings are the most fertile source in Scripture about Mary and Jesus.
- Part two offers meditations on Mary's relationship to Christ in his public ministry.
- Part three considers Mary's participation in Christ's Passion, Death, Resurrection, and sending of the Holy Spirit.

How to Use This Book

Holding Jesus is an ideal resource for anyone who already has or wants to cultivate a deep relationship and understanding of Mary as the Mother of God. I suggest that you consider the meditations in part one as nourishment for your Advent-to-Christmas spiritual renewal. Parts two and three can become your spiritual food during Ordinary Time and Lent. Of course, you should feel free to adopt these reflections for your prayer and reflection at any time of the year.

Each of the forty-two reflections in *Holding Jesus* offers Scripture to ponder, an inspirational quote, and a brief meditation whose first half is derived from a scriptural reading and whose second half, most of the time, is devoted to aspects of Mary's relationship with her Son.

I conclude the meditations with a prayer and a question that applies the teaching to your daily life. Finally, I have tried with these meditations to involve you in some way through stories, images, or familiar acts of piety.

Holding Jesus, while certainly appropriate for personal use, would also be a valuable prayer resource for Bible study groups, book clubs, women's or men's groups, small faith-sharing communities, and so on. One person in such groups could act as leader and read or ask for volunteer readers to speak aloud the different parts of the reflection. The question could provide a starting point for group discussion and faith sharing.

I am grateful to the staff of Franciscan Media, and especially to Lisa Biedenbach, one of its directors of product development, for suggesting Mary as Mother of God as a topic for a book.

May Mary hold them—and you—close to her heart.

PART ONE

Holding the Child Jesus

"Come, let us worship the Lord, the King who is to come."

With these words the Church invites us to prepare our hearts to receive the newborn Jesus with greater humility, affection, and faith. The mysteries of the liturgy make it possible for us to be present to the history and process by which the Word became flesh and dwelt among us for our salvation. Through the celebration of the liturgical seasons such as Advent, we have the honor of being in touch with the generations of faith both in the Old Testament and the New Testament. Far from being merely ancient history, the liturgy makes present the details of the mystery of God's plan to save us and invites us to adopt the energy of the faith of our mothers and fathers from the dawn of life.

The *Catechism of the Catholic Church* explains this truth in the following way: "When the Church celebrates the liturgy of Advent each year, she makes present this ancient expectancy of the Messiah, for by sharing in the long preparation for the Savior's first coming, the faithful renew their ardent desire for his second coming…. Christian liturgy not only recalls the events that saved us, but actualizes them, makes them present" (*CCC,* 524, 1104).

In the reflections of part one, I approach the mysteries of Advent from the viewpoint of Mary's essential role in preparing for Christ's birth. It is Mary who lived and practiced the first Advent. Mary is the key figure in the birth of Jesus. Not only does she prepare for his birth like any pregnant mother, but she possesses the fervor of a woman of faith who approaches her maternity with a sense of wonder and gratitude for being the remarkable instrument of God's eternal plan to save us from sin and death and provide us with the gift of divine life. It is hardly an exaggeration to say that Mary's maternal preparation for Christ's birth is unique among all the billions of births of history.

First Sunday of Advent
Wait With Mary for Christ's Coming

READINGS

Isaiah 2:1–5 — Come, let us climb the Lord's mountain, that he may instruct us in his way.

Romans 13:11–14 — Let us throw off the works of darkness...and put on the Lord Jesus Christ.

Matthew 24:37–44 — Be prepared, for at an hour you do not expect, the Son of Man will come.

INSPIRATIONAL QUOTE

I sing a maid of tender years
to whom an angel came
And knelt as to a mighty queen,
and bowed his wings of flame;
A nation's hope in her reply,
this maid of matchless grace;
For God's own Son became her child,
and she his resting place.

—"I Sing a Maid"[1]

REFLECTION

Before Mary heard the angel's message that she would be the Mother of the Messiah, she often heard the words of Isaiah read at synagogue. She listened to the rabbi speak passionately about the coming of the Messiah. Sitting in the women's space behind the wooden screen she pondered Isaiah's prediction that a virgin would conceive and bear a son who would be called Emmanuel, God-with-us, never dreaming this would be her vocation (see Isaiah 7:14). With a heart that yearned for peace she prayed for the day when the Messiah would turn swords into plowshares and spears into hooks for pruning vines. After the angel invited her to accept God's will, in her pregnancy she lived months waiting for the coming of her messianic child.

At the cross, Mary's Son entrusted her to John. Tradition says that John brought her with him to Ephesus. Scripture says that Paul preached in Ephesus for two years. We can imagine him visiting Mary and John as he preached. What he wrote to the Romans would also be central to his preaching in Ephesus, though difficult for his crowds to accept. "Let us live honorably as in the day, not in reveling and drunkenness, not in debauchery and licentiousness, not in quarreling and jealousy…. Instead, put on the Lord Jesus" (Romans 13:13–14). Mary knew all too well the failures of human nature she witnessed in her years in Nazareth. As we relive through the liturgy of Advent the coming of Jesus, let us pray to Mary that we do this with faith, patience, and a resolve to be more fervent in our moral lives.

QUESTION

What is one way in which I will prepare my heart for Christ's coming?

PRAYER

Lord, in the spirit of Isaiah we yearn for Christ's coming. We pray that, with Mary's intercession, we will banish evil from our hearts and seek always what is good and just. We praise you, Lord, for the opportunity to think of you during our advent journey with Mary.

Monday of the First Week of Advent
Learn From the Humility of a Soldier

READINGS

Isaiah 4:2–6   God purified his people.

Matthew 8:5–11   Many will come from east to west into the Kingdom of heaven.

INSPIRATIONAL QUOTE

Mary dear, remember me,
And never cease your care,
Till in heaven eternally,
Your love and bliss I share.
—Variation of "Mother Dear, Oh, Pray for Me"[2]

REFLECTION

Most people are touched by an experience of humility. Spiritual writers acclaim humility as the root of all the virtues. Today's Gospel tells of a centurion who comes to Christ begging a cure for his servant. Jesus agrees to go to the man's house to do it. Humbly, the soldier says, "Lord, I am not worthy to have you come under my roof; but only speak the word, and my servant will be healed" (Matthew 8:8). Jesus is amazed by the humble faith of the man. Our Lord uses this case as a forecast of salvation for the world for many will come from east and west to rest in the bosom of Abraham, the father of faith as the Catechism says. It is often remarked that we use the centurion's prayer when we receive the Eucharist.

In her Magnificat, Mary sings of the blessings of her humility, "My soul magnifies the Lord...for he has looked with favor on the lowliness of his servant" (Luke 1:47–48). For our personal preparation for a renewal of Christ we need a renewal of the virtue of humility. Virtues are usually acquired by being inspired by a virtuous person, such as the centurion or Mary. Good example is contagious. Virtue is also gained by repetition of virtuous acts. Real virtue grooves the soul. Of course, all virtue requires graces from God, all the better when Mary intercedes for us.

QUESTION

How strong is my attraction to humility? What must I do?

PRAYER

Jesus, we want to accept your invitation, "Come to me, all you that are weary and carrying heavy burdens.... Learn from me; for I am gentle and humble in heart, and you will find rest for your souls" (Matthew 11:28–29). As you say, this is a learning experience. Teach us how. As Jesus grew in wisdom under your training, O blessed Mary, give us your motherly wisdom.

Dream of Peace With the Spirit

READINGS

Isaiah 11:1–10   The Spirit of the Lord shall rest on the Messiah.

Luke 10:21–24   Jesus reveals he is the one on whom the Spirit rests.

INSPIRATIONAL QUOTE

You and your Mother, Lord, are the only perfectly beautiful ones…. There was no stain of sin in your Mother.

—St. Ephrem of Syria[3]

REFLECTION

We are a strange people. We feel militant when a war begins. Weary with war, we sigh when peace is declared. On a wedding day we share the promise of a bride and groom who seem ready to love each other forever. We mourn when, all too often, they break up. Who would fail to smile when a baby is born? Who could brush away a tear when a calamity strikes that child? Promise and fulfillment continue to enchant us. Reality rains on our parade. Isaiah prophesied that the Spirit of God would rest on the Messiah. The result would be glorious—peace for everyone. Even the lion would snuggle with a lamb. A baby will play by a cobra's den. This is an inspired dream that is possible, if only the world would really accept Jesus and let him work his peace-filled and powerful graces on our hearts. The dream is necessary. But we must wake up.

Let's take a little walk with Mary in her neighborhood of Nazareth. She is pregnant with the desired of all nations. The town is quiet as people take an afternoon siesta. Mary is filled with the afterglow of a vision of an angel. Her faith is firm because she spoke a world-changing "yes." The dream is vivid. But already she worries. What will Joseph think? Will an angel tell him? How will the neighbors react? In these mixed feelings, Mary experiences the continued presence of God. Somehow in the silence, she hears, "Trust me." That's just what she did.

Mary, teach me in my own confusion in a mixed-up world how to trust in God. Tell me that surrender to God is the best spiritual medicine.

QUESTION

When have I said "yes" to God? How would I describe my faith at that time?

PRAYER

Lord Jesus, we rejoice in the dream of peace the Spirit works in you. We hunger for peace in our families, neighborhoods, and world. Yet, we are mixed up, torn between idealism and our personal failures. Take our hearts and heal them. Mother Mary, show us the way to inner peace.

Dine at Christ's Table

READINGS

Isaiah 25:6–10   God invites us to his dinner table.

Matthew 15:29–37   Jesus hosts a messianic banquet.

**INSPIRATIONAL
QUOTE**

> The Blessed Virgin does not disillusion any of the profound expectations of the men and women of our time. She offers us a perfect model of a disciple of the Lord.
>
> —Pope Paul VI[4]

REFLECTION

Most people like to be invited out to dinner. Many would swoon over being asked to dine with a world-famous celebrity. In a simpler way, one of life's greatest pleasures is a good meal with family and friends. God's gifts are built upon the basics of the human condition such as table fellowship. Jesus hosted a messianic banquet with a bread miracle. The four thousand guests were so excited they sought to make him a king. Jesus smiled at their childish desire. He would lift the event from a roadside lunch to a sacrament at the Last Supper. Today his meal is now the Eucharist, the Bread of Angels, his real saving presence for our salvation. He invites us to dine at his table. "Behold, I stand at the door and knock. If anyone hears my voice and opens the door, I will come in to him and eat with him, and he with me" (Revelation 3:20–21, *RSV*). Mary hosted messianic meals every day for more than thirty years. The guest of honor was the Word made flesh. The real presence of Jesus was historically at her table. After the Resurrection, Mary would receive Jesus in the Eucharist. We cannot count all the years Mary enjoyed table fellowship with the Messiah, but one thing is sure—it was never routine for her. Mary experienced a profound union with the real presence of Jesus as a child, a young man, and a savior whose messianic ministry involved death and resurrection.

Mary, come with me when I go to Mass. Help me fold my hands with reverence and open my heart with faith so Jesus and I can have table fellowship.

QUESTION

How have I overcome my participation in the Mass becoming routine?

PRAYER

O Lord, we join the Church in hailing you as the Messiah long hoped for by God's people in the Old Testament. We know we are lax in having a personal devotion to you as really present to us at Mass. Mary, please curb our curious minds that wander so much. Claim us as attentive disciples.

Staying Faithful in Tough Times

READINGS

Isaiah 26:1–6   God says, "Keep the faith!"

Matthew 7:21,   Build your faith on the solid rock of Christ.
17–24

**INSPIRATIONAL
QUOTE**

If the winds of temptation arise,

…look to the star, call on Mary

If anger or avarice…assail the vessel of your soul,

look at the star, call upon Mary.

—St. Bernard of Clairvaux[5]

REFLECTION

Personal faith is an odd sort of thing. The God in whom we have faith is an eternal rock. Yet a lot of believers have built their faith on sand. Somehow they missed the point. Their God is a moveable target. In the book of Revelation, the letter to the Laodiceans starkly describes the frail faith of some believers. They hear a sharp rebuke from Christ. "I know your works: you are neither cold nor hot.… So, because you are lukewarm, and neither cold nor hot, I am about to spit you out of my mouth" (Revelation 3:15–16). Christ sounds stern here. More exasperated than angry, he wants believers with strong commitment.

This is shake-up time. Christ wants rocks, not sand. How can he build a kingdom with sideliners? Advent is a call for enduring fidelity. Christ's pointed remarks are medicinal. He wants to heal us.

Catholic devotion sometimes seems to reduce Mary to a sentimental woman. She's anything but. She bore Jesus in a cold cave. She made a rocky flight to a foreign land to save her Son. She braved the jeers of her Son's enemies in the Passion. She was tough. Catholic devotion to Our Lady of Sorrows is more than an emotional picture of Mary. It is a painful, yet inspiring, look into the life of a woman who really knew there is no love without sacrifice.

Mary, put some spine in my faith.

QUESTION

Is my faith weak like sand or strong like a rock?

PRAYER

In reflecting on our faith we take some courage from an old hymn: "On Christ, the solid rock I stand. All other ground is sinking sand." We know we must overcome settling for less in our commitment to you, our God. To take the road of least resistance will reduce our faith to mere externalism. O Blessed Mother, show us the road to courage. Mary, valiant Lady, arouse within us a heroic attitude toward our faith in Christ. Catholic martyrs from the days of the early Church to modern times stood up for their faith. It's never too late to believe.

FRIDAY OF THE FIRST WEEK OF ADVENT

Believing Is Seeing

READINGS

Isaiah 29:17–24   When the Messiah comes, the blind will see.

Matthew 9:27–31   Because they believed in Jesus, the blind were cured.

INSPIRATIONAL
QUOTE

> Can a mother forget her nursing-child,
>   or show no compassion for the child of her
>   womb?
> Even these may forget,
>   yet I will not forget you.
> See, I have inscribed you on the palms of my
>   hands.
>
> —Isaiah 49:15–16

REFLECTION

Everyday wisdom says, "Seeing is believing." Middle America says, "Show me. I'm from Missouri." This is the world of reason and science. The world of faith reverses the proverb by stating, "Believing is seeing." Pope Benedict XVI often says, "Faith is a way of knowing or seeing spiritual truths." There is no contradiction between the two paths. Truth is truth whether perceived by reason or faith. God is the origin of truth whether scientific or revealed. Isaiah calls his people to believe that when the Messiah comes, "The eyes of the blind will see."

Jesus advises the blind men to believe in him so they will regain sight. The triumphs of the Internet, Facebook, and YouTube flood our eyes with billions of instant impressions. It causes visual weariness and distracts us from faith's eyesight. Balance this with the wisdom of the psalmist, "I have set my soul in silence and peace. As a child rests in his mother's arms, even so my soul rests in you my God."[6]

As a woman of faith, Mary is an outstanding believer. When Scripture wonders whether a mother could forget her child or be without compassion for the child in her womb, the answer is that God could never forget the infant. Mary's immense faith would never dream of forgetting Jesus or losing compassion for him in her womb. The world today has canonized blindly forgetting the child in the womb. Mary disagrees. She is right, "Believing is seeing." Only the recovery of faith will save the children.

Holy Mary, pray for the innocents.

QUESTION

How well do I understand that faith is a path to knowing truth?

PRAYER

Compassionate Jesus, lead us to a faith that gives truth to our minds and love to our hearts. You performed miracles for those who understood they needed faith in you so their healing could happen. Impressive as that was, our forthcoming celebration of your birth will be a festival of light. You are our light and salvation. We would like a Christmas present that enables us to live near you all the days of our lives. Let us gaze on your loveliness so that our fears will be cast out because of the gift of your love.

Saturday of the First Week of Advent
Mercy Flows From Heaven Above

READINGS

Isaiah 30:19–21, 23–26   The Messiah will bind up the wounds of his people.

Matthew 9:35— 10:1, 5a, 6–8   At the sight of the crowd, Christ was moved with pity for them.

INSPIRATIONAL QUOTE

Teach me to feel another's woe,
To hide the fault I see.
That mercy I to others show
That mercy show to me.

—Alexander Pope[7]

REFLECTION

Poets and philosophers make mercy a divine value because it is so often missing among humans. To be unforgiving is human. To show mercy is divine. Shakespeare says that kings are supposed to be noted for dispensing justice. But mercy becomes the monarch better than his crown. Matthew describes Jesus having pity on the crowds that follow him because they were troubled and abandoned like sheep without a shepherd. Not only do we need more shepherds today, but we need ones who lead our people with hearts full of mercy. Why do so many people find it hard to be merciful? Because they spend too much time licking their own wounds and examining the motives of those who injured them. Mercy is the gentle rain that blesses him or her who gives it—and the one who receives it. This causes the growth of new and richer friendships. By the way, an apology is a good way to have the last word.

One of the most beautiful developments of the history of the Church's devotion to Mary is her title "Mother of Mercy." As she stood by the cross, she heard her Son forgive his enemies. She had taught him that as a child. Most of us retain fond memories of our mothers as the locus of family forgiveness. So it is not surprising that we turn to our Blessed Mother for access to divine mercy. One thing is certain, Mary is the Queen of Heaven and our supreme intercessor with her beloved Son.

Mary, in this Advent, fold your arms of mercy around me so that I can become a forgiving person.

QUESTION

How have I overcome my failures to forgive others?

PRAYER

O come, divine Messiah, bring to us the treasure of your mercy so that we may receive it and bestow it on others. Your gracious power to forgive has shaped Christianity for over two thousand years. We would love to be able to forget and forgive real and imagined slights and offenses. What a privilege that would be!

SECOND SUNDAY OF ADVENT

Through the Messiah We Come to Know the Spirit

READINGS

Isaiah 11:1–10	The Messiah will be filled with the gifts of the Holy Spirit.
Romans 15:4–9	Paul prays that God will help the Romans think in harmony with each other.
Matthew 3:1–12	The Baptist preaches that Christ will baptize us in the Spirit.

INSPIRATIONAL QUOTE

Come down, O Love divine,

seek now this soul of mine,

And visit it with your own ardor glowing;

O Comforter, draw near,

Within my heart appear,

And kindle it, your holy flame bestowing.

—"Come Down, O Love Divine"[8]

REFLECTION

Today our Advent journey links the Holy Spirit to the life and saving ministry of Jesus. "The spirit of the LORD shall rest upon him, / a spirit of wisdom and understanding" (Isaiah 11:2). The Old Testament provides images of the Holy Spirit in stories of God's breath. "The LORD God formed man from the dust of the ground, and breathed into his nostrils the breath of life" (Genesis 2:7). God's breath gave the prophets a social conscience and a mission of spiritual renewal. Ezekiel saw a valley of dry bones. Could they live again? He prayed for God's creative breath. Ezekiel proclaimed, "Come from the four winds, O breath, and breathe upon these slain, that they may live" (Ezekiel 37:9). And they came to life. The Messiah sends the Holy Spirit who will transform the dry bones of our fatigued faith into hearts on fire with joy and love.

On a peaceful afternoon in Nazareth, Mary experienced her first profound meeting with the Holy Spirit. She had surrendered to God's will. In the silence of her body the Spirit created the beginning of her child. Such a mystery will never be surpassed. She heard again Gabriel's words, "The Holy Spirit will come upon you...the child to be born will be holy; he will be called Son of God" (Luke 1:35). Later, when her cousin Elizabeth heard Mary's greeting, she felt little John leap in her womb. Filled with the Holy Spirit, she cried out with a very loud voice and said, "Blessed are you among women, and blessed is the fruit of your womb…. Blessed is she who believed that there would be a fulfillment of what was spoken to her by the Lord" (Luke 1:42, 45). Ever since that moment we have called Mary our Blessed Mother.

Holy Mary, Mother of God, pray for me.

QUESTION

In what way has the Holy Spirit affected my spirituality?

PRAYER

Come, Holy Spirit, into our lives. Fill our hearts with the joy that belongs to your very being. Teach us to sing the blessings you have offered us throughout our lives. Focus our eyes on Jesus from whom every saving grace comes. Move us from a fatigued faith to a living faith.

Monday of the Second Week of Advent
Spiritual Wellness

READINGS

Isaiah 35:1–10   Strengthen the hands that are feeble. Make firm the knees that are weak.

Luke 5:17–26   One day while Jesus was teaching, the power of the Lord was with him.

**INSPIRATIONAL
QUOTE**

The King of glory comes, the nation rejoices;
Open the gates before him, lift up your voices.
In all of Galilee, in city or village,
He goes among his people curing their illness.

—W.F. Jabusch[9]

REFLECTION

In our times we have rediscovered some old truths about being healthy. We are reminded that our attitude is essential to health. We are told that a good diet needs to be accompanied by regular physical exercise and a positive mental attitude. Health is the result of a total plan that repairs inner attitudes as well as attention to the body. Wellness centers (or their equivalent) have emerged to treat the whole person. Wellness ideas meet our psychological and physical needs. Jesus goes further and heals our spiritual and moral needs. Delivery from moral evil is as important as delivery from emotional and physical illness. The Messiah strengthens the hands that are feeble and the knees that are weak. For our moral growth he forgives our sins.

When Joachim and Anne beheld their little girl, Mary, they would not have known her destiny or the remarkable state of her soul. Doubtless they were pleased with Mary's character, moral purity, and devotion to God. God had a total plan for Mary, for her wellness in the complete sense. God prepared her to be the Mother of the Messiah. When someone praised Jesus by praising his Mother, he curiously said that those who hear the Word of God and keep it are his mother, brother, and sister. Actually, he was saying that the only one who did this was Mary. No wonder the Eastern Churches call Mary "Panagia," the all-holy one.

Mother Mary, hold me close to your Immaculate Heart. Treat me as one of your children. Guide me on the path of Christ's version of wellness.

QUESTION

In what way have I followed a plan for total wellness?

PRAYER

Good Shepherd, you are the kind of leader who works with our potential and seeks to open us up to what you know we can and should become. May we learn to lead those we must in the way you would do it. We praise you for the trust you inspire in us to follow you, allowing us to discover who we are meant to be.

**Without God's Son, Nothing Could Exist;
Without Mary's Son, Nothing Could Be
Redeemed.**

—St. Anselm[10]

READINGS

Genesis 3:9–15, 20	The story of the Fall of Adam and Eve.
Ephesians 1:3–6, 11–12	God chose us in his Son to be holy and without blemish.
Luke 1:26–38	Hail Mary "Full of Grace."

INSPIRATIONAL

QUOTE

O Mother, how pure you are, you are untouched by sin; yours was the privilege to carry God within you.

—Liturgy of the Hours, Morning Prayer, December 8[11]

REFLECTION

If you make pilgrimage to Lourdes in the summertime, one of your greatest moments will be the evening candlelight procession. You will hold a lighted candle and walk with an enormous crowd and sing,

"Immaculate Mary, your praises we sing. You reign now in heaven with Jesus our king. Ave Maria (Hail Mary)." Millions go there every year, some seeking a miracle cure, all looking for a revival of their hope and faith. Mary does not disappoint you. Of course, faith is required. The opening words of the film *The Song of Bernadette* consider this mystery: "To those who believe, no explanation is necessary. To those who do not believe, no explanation will suffice." Devotion to Mary leads us to love for Jesus. Her whole life was dedicated with a passion to Jesus. Her last words in the Bible were, "Do what he [Jesus] tells you" (John 2:5).

It is a stroke of genius for the Church to place Mary's Immaculate Conception in Advent. Her feast dwells on her conception. Christmas focuses on her Son's birth. A sinless woman begets a sinless child. St. Anselm says that without God's Son nothing could exist. Then smiling at Mary, he writes that no one could be saved without Mary's Son. We join the angels and saints that sing God's blessings given to her. I love Wordsworth's line that says Mary is "our tainted nature's solitary boast." Despite her incredible gift, she prefers to stress humility in her reply to the angel Gabriel: "Here am I, the servant of the Lord" (Luke 1:38).

Holy Mother, say a little prayer for me today that I may let God give me sanctity.

QUESTION

What kind of relationship do I have with Mary?

PRAYER

Jesus, we join you in celebrating this feast of your Mother. Trace in our hearts the lines of her love and her readiness of faith. As our years go by, with her prayers may we finally have the humility to belong to you alone. With the angels we sing, *Ave Maria.*

You Will Run and Not Grow Weary

READINGS

Isaiah 40:25–31   Our strong God gives strength to the weary.

Matthew 11:28–30   Jesus provides rest and renewal for the burdened.

**INSPIRATIONAL
QUOTE**

He will feed his flock like a shepherd;
   He will gather the lambs in his arms,
and carry them in his bosom,
   and gently lead the mother sheep.

—Isaiah 40:11

REFLECTION

The film *Chariots of Fire* tells the story of two young men who compete in the Paris Olympics in 1924. One is a Scot who plans to be a missionary to China. The other is an English Jewish student at Cambridge. The missionary wants to win a medal in honor of his Christian faith. The other desires to prove himself against the anti-Semitism he experiences. They each overcome obstacles. The Christian refuses to run on Sunday out of respect for the Sabbath. The Jewish man loses several preparatory trial runs. Discouraged he says, "I won't run if I can't win." His girlfriend says, "You won't win if you don't run." Both men persist and win medals. One of the highlights features the Scot at Sunday services reading Isaiah 40 with pictures of runners falling in mud and getting up. Our heroes both have a religious passion that God's words confirm.

One of Mary's most discouraging moments was walking with her Son on his march to the cross. Her heart is stung as he falls in the mud several times and struggles up again. Jesus remembers his Father's words: "Those who wait for the LORD / shall renew their strength, / they shall mount up with wings like eagles" (Isaiah 40:31). Mary knows those words as well. Together with Jesus she pulls herself along and draws power from God's throne and her Son's courage. Neither of them received Olympic medals. But Mary obtained the greatest medal ever seen in the world, won by her Son—the promised salvation to all to believe and desire to be saved.

Courageous Mary, give me even one-millionth of the bravery you showed in that walk to the cross. When I faint and grow weary, when I stagger and fall, pick me up and say, "Get going!"

QUESTION

How has God helped me soar with eagle's wings after falls and sufferings?

PRAYER

Bless the Lord, O my soul. Thank you, God, for forgiving our sins and healing our hearts when we have walked away from you. We are grateful that you are slow to anger and abounding in kindness. In our life's race to our destiny we ask you to crown us with kindness and compassion. With you and Mary we dream of soaring toward you on eagle's wings.

John the Baptist Is the Voice—
Jesus Is the Word

READINGS

Isaiah 41:13–20	I the Lord say to you, "Fear not, I will help you."
Matthew 11:11–15	The least in the kingdom is greater than he (John the Baptist).

INSPIRATIONAL QUOTE

Angels and archangels may have gathered there,
Cherubim and seraphim thronged the air;
But His mother only, in her maiden bliss,
Worshipped the beloved with a kiss.

—Christina Rossetti[12]

REFLECTION

When John the Baptist began his preaching ministry, his listeners were thrilled. Here at last, after four centuries, God had sent them a real live prophet. So excited were some people that they thought John was the Messiah. But John denied this, claiming he was God's messenger announcing the arrival of the Messiah. St. Augustine compared John's voice to Christ as the Word. He said that John's voice lasted only for a while. Christ who is the Word made flesh will last forever.

The reason John was so effective was that his voice was filled with Christ the Word. The voice without the word touches the ear, but fails to move the heart. Augustine told his congregation that he searched for a way to share with their hearts what was in his heart. Cardinal Newman expressed Augustine's point in his motto, *Cor ad cor loquitur* ("My heart speaks to your heart"). What is the Word? Jesus is God's Word of infinite love.

As we walk with Mary through Advent, we marvel at how completely she united her heart to God's. After all, she is carrying the Word made flesh within her. She had been touched by God. In a sense she is also touching God. Her union with her child is both physical and spiritual. When he is born she could "worship the beloved with a kiss" as Christina Rossetti wrote in the verse above. Gazing at this remarkable scene, St. Ambrose is moved to coin a sentence that rings more true than ever today. "Christian, remember your dignity." God chose to honor human beings with his intimate union with humanity and purify us from sin. An innocent mother will soon kiss the supremely innocent baby. Now that's really heart speaking to the heart!

Mother Mary, show me how to pray with my heart to Christ's heart.

QUESTION

How well have I learned to appreciate my human dignity as a gift from Christ?

PRAYER

Holy Spirit, who leads us to prayer, help us to recognize the love you offer us. Awaken our souls to the mystery of Word made flesh in the womb of Mary. Purify our hearts so we can prepare for a fresh coming of Christ into our lives.

FRIDAY OF THE SECOND WEEK OF ADVENT
The Best Way to Listen to God Is to Pray

READINGS

Isaiah 48:17–19   If you listened to my commandments your descendants would be like a river.

Matthew 11:16–19   The people listened to neither John nor Christ.

INSPIRATIONAL
QUOTE

Escape from your everyday business for a short while, hide for a moment from your restless thoughts. Break off from your cares and troubles.... Make a little time for God and rest a while in him.

Enter into your mind's inner chamber. Shut out everything but God...and when you have shut the door, look for him.

—St. Anselm[13]

REFLECTION

St. Anselm (1033–1109) was a mountain boy who left the Alps when he was twenty-one. A restless young man, he roamed around France for three years. Then he settled in the Abbey of Bec where he matured under the guidance of Abbot Lanfranc. He became a philosopher and also a man of deep prayer. His writings on prayer influenced all classes of people. He is read by the Church today as part of our preparation for Christmas. The Scripture readings reveal a perennial problem for people of faith, namely, the capacity to listen to God. Anselm's practical advice is that the best way to hear God is to be quiet and pray. Even in the quiet of rural, medieval France this counsel was needed. Conversely, in the noise of our digital culture and fast-track business, Anselm's words mean more to us than ever.

While we journey with Mary toward Christmas, we note how few words of Mary are recorded in Scripture. Her longest passage was the one she sang in her Magnificat where she praised God for the glorious gift she has received as Mother of God. This does not prove she had little to say. What she did utter has always been a treasure for us. Scripture reveals her as a profound woman who contemplates in her heart the events of salvation wrought by her Son. She approaches them quietly. If we would like to know how to acquire the gift of silence, we should listen to Mary. By not saying much she shows us the pleasures of slowing down our tongues and allowing our souls to thrive. Chatterboxes could benefit with such a discipline. Being talkative is not evil, but it prevents us from hearing God's wisdom, which is so beneficial for our peace of heart.

Blessed woman of silence, teach us the prayer of quiet so we can hear God.

QUESTION

What does my living environment need to be more peaceful and quiet?

PRAYER

Jesus, we hear again your words about playing a flute, but the listeners did not dance, and we hear your words about singing a dirge, but no one mourned. You chose a rather humorous way to help us learn that the best way to hear you is to pray. We would welcome from you the graces of prayer.

Saturday of the Second Week of Advent
Our Lady of Guadalupe as the Star of Evangelization

READINGS

Revelation 11:19a; 12:1–6a, 10ab

A great sign appeared in the sky.

Luke 1:26–38

May it be done unto me according to your word.

INSPIRATIONAL QUOTE

Once in Royal David's city
Stood a lowly cattle shed,
Where a mother laid her baby
In a manger for his bed.
Mary was that mother mild,
Jesus Christ, her little child.

—Cecil Frances Alexander[14]

REFLECTION

On December 12, 1531, our Blessed Mother appeared to a convert named Juan Diego. She left him with an image imprinted upon his cloak. The image may now be seen in a magnificent shrine in Mexico City. The growth of devotion to her inspired a dynamic increase of conversion to Christianity among the indigenous population. Today she is honored as the patroness of the Americas. With the dramatic increase of Latino

Catholics in the United States, devotion to her has been a great help for them to sustain their Catholic faith while integrating themselves into our country. In historic terms, going to Mary is a sure step to union with Jesus. All over our land the vigil of Our Lady of Guadalupe is a joyful and festive celebration of her love and destiny.

At Christmas, Mary gave us Jesus. She has never stopped doing that. Pope Paul VI called her the "Star of Evangelization." Like the star that led the Magi to Christ, Mary continues to be the star that draws each of us to Jesus. The original Guadalupe image of Mary was amplified with a golden sunburst around her. This artistic touch identified her with the vision of the "woman clothed with the sun, with the moon under her feet," as described in Revelation 12:1 and serving as the First Reading in today's liturgy. Her shrine in Mexico City attracts over ten million pilgrims each year. As Pope Benedict calls us to the "New Evangelization," we should invoke Mary under her many titles. She loves bringing her Son to us.

Mary of the Americas, help us attract millions to Christ.

QUESTION
How much do I need to increase my friendship with Mary?

PRAYER
O Virgin Mary of Guadalupe, we invoke your prayers to help all people accept each other as brothers and sisters. May your Son's peace be spread throughout the world.

Jesus Used the Proof of Joy as the Sign of His Messiahship

READINGS

Isaiah 35:1–6a, 10	When the Messiah comes we will see the joyful glory of the Lord.
James 5:7–10	Make your hearts joyful because the coming of the Lord is at hand.
Matthew 11:2–11	Joyful are those who take no offense in Christ.

INSPIRATIONAL
QUOTE

Go tell it on the mountain

Over the hills and everywhere,

Go tell it on the mountain,

Our Jesus Christ is born.

—Hymn for the Christmas Season[15]

REFLECTION

Jesuit Father James Martin has written a book about the role of joy in our religion. Its title, *Between Heaven and Mirth,* is a pun that puts a smile on our faces as soon as we hear it. The cover itself is amusing, showing Mother Teresa, John Paul II, Benedict XVI, St. Francis, St. Ignatius, and others, all laughing. He takes fun seriously. He has written a humorous book that makes the Third Sunday of Advent's theme of joy come alive. When Christianity is fresh and new and properly understood, it makes people joyful. Jesus used the "proof of joy" in the message he sent to John the Baptist. The happy blind see. The joyful lame walk. The cleansed lepers are ecstatic. The poor have the good/happy news proclaimed to them. The opening words of the Mass make it clear. "Rejoice in the Lord always; again I will say, Rejoice. The Lord is near" (Philippians 4:4–5).

Mary leaps for joy when she hears Elizabeth's good news. Elizabeth is smiling as she feels the child in her womb jumping for joy upon hearing Mary's greeting. While Scripture seems a bit too reverent to think of fun or a joke, we still might say that Mary and others knew a divine sense of humor. In order to laugh at a joke we must see the point. God has made the world in such a way that he is the point of all we see. All sins are missing the point. (The Hebrew word for *sin* means "missing the mark.") We Christians are meant to have a sense of humor. That is why we have a better chance of getting the point of creation. We can smile because we know how to cry. We can laugh because we know how to suffer. We can see God because we get the whole point of it all.

Dear Mary and Elizabeth, pray that we have a sense of humor.

QUESTION

How did I learn to be joyful and have a sense of humor?

PRAYER

Father of happiness, give us wit along with our worldly wisdom so we can be open to the joyful surprises you constantly prepare for us. Rescue us from too much solemnity that our joy may be pure and growing.

Monday of the Third Week of Advent
The Heavens Declare the Glory of God

READINGS

Numbers 24:2–7, 15–17   A star shall advance from Jacob.

Matthew 21:23–27   Chief priests ask Jesus, "By what authority are you doing these things?"

INSPIRATIONAL QUOTE

Oh, star of wonder, star of night,
Star with royal beauty bright.
Westward leading, still proceeding,
Guide us to the perfect Light.

—John H. Hopkins, Jr.[16]

REFLECTION

In the TV special *A Charlie Brown Christmas,* Linus recites Luke's Gospel account of the birth of Jesus. While he is reading, he lets go of his security blanket. He finds his security in God's Word. The birth of Jesus elevates human nature to the possibilities of resting in the power of an infinite and loving God. Little children fearfully hold onto their blankets and suck their thumbs. Adults seek the same solace in money, sex, alcohol, drugs, and power. It works for a while, but it doesn't last. Only the longing for God provides the security that satisfies us. God's Word is the safest blanket. The birth of Jesus is said to occur at night. Angels of light sing his praises. A star at night brings about the Adoration of the Magi. We can only see the stars at night. Dark times in our lives make it possible to see God's light. Even our troubles have silver linings.

We have already noted that Pope Paul VI called Mary the "Star of Evangelization." While astronomy has unfolded the science of these heavenly appearances, there is no way this will eliminate the mystique of stars and moon. Spiritual writers have compared Mary to the moon, which derives its light from the sun, which symbolizes the radiance of Jesus. When Mary appeared to Sr. Catherine Labouré, she wore a crown of stars and stood on the moon. This scene was transferred to what became known as the Miraculous Medal. The meaning was spelled out in the prayer, "O Mary, conceived without sin, pray for us who have recourse to thee." It has become one of the most popular devotional medals of all time.

Dear Mary Immaculate, heavenly star, shine your light of Jesus into our souls.

QUESTION

How can I drop my own "security blanket" and lean fully on Jesus?

PRAYER

Immaculate Mary, pray that we clear away the foolish security blankets that we use to avoid abandoning ourselves to Christ. Help us to be convinced that the soundest investment of our energies is the gold standard of Jesus. We should learn that we can only see the stars when life is dark. We will treasure our spiritual nights to see you, our motherly star of wonder.

Jesus Is Close to the Brokenhearted

READINGS

Zephaniah 3:1–2, 9–13	I will leave in your midst a people humble and lowly.
Matthew 21:28–32	The Lord is close to the brokenhearted.

INSPIRATIONAL QUOTE

The Word is visible to the heart alone, while flesh is visible to bodily eyes as well…. We had no means of seeing the Word. The Word was made flesh so we could see it.

—St. Augustine[17]

REFLECTION

Each morning in St. Paul, Minnesota, Mary Jo goes to her parish church at 4 AM and begins two hours of prayer before attending Mass. Then she goes to the passion of her life, ministering to the brokenhearted. She oversees a food pantry for the homeless that provides breakfast and showers, along with free dental and medical care. There is a sign-up sheet for the washing of the feet—twenty are treated each afternoon. She kneels before them, knowing that many pull back from human touch because they have experienced so much rejection. Crossing the street she goes to the day care floor for the little ones, then to the gym for the teens. Finally she checks the apartment house that offers six-month terms for homeless families to get them on their feet. With loads of volunteers, her faith-based efforts prosper with low overhead, love for those they serve, and commitment to mending the brokenhearted.

Born poor and verbally abused by her father, who told her, "You'll never amount to anything," she married a loving man. He understood her and supported her remarkable ministry for the brokenhearted after they raised a large family of their own. Our Blessed Mother is her patroness who supports her with an abundance of Christ's graces. Adoration of the Blessed Sacrament and Mass are the "fireplace" that warms her up for the day ahead. In Advent we hear repeatedly from the prophets that the future Messiah will heal broken hearts. The Lord hears the cry of the poor, especially through people like Mary Jo who invoke our Blessed Mother for daily help.

Dear Mother Mary, teach us Christ's way to mend hearts.

QUESTION

How have I dealt with broken hearts in my family and elsewhere?

PRAYER

Jesus, your heart was pierced when you were dying for love of us so we could be saved from our sins. Your sacred heart is a huge spiritual resource for us and millions of others. May we live by your words, "Blessed are the pure of heart. They shall see God."

Banish Injustice With Humble Love

READINGS

Isaiah 45:6c–8, 18–21c, 25	Let justice descend from the heavens.
Luke 7:18b–23	Tell John what you have seen and heard.

INSPIRATIONAL QUOTE

At some thoughts a man stands perplexed, above all at the sight of human sin, and he wonders whether to combat it by force or by humble love. Always decide: "I will combat it by humble love." If you resolve on that once for all, you can conquer the whole world. Loving humility is a terrible force: it is the strongest of all things, and there is nothing else like it.

—Fyodor Dostoevsky[18]

REFLECTION

Today we hear Isaiah , with his passion for a messiah, virtually shouting, "Shower, O heavens, from above, / and let the skies rain down righteousness/ ... / Only in the LORD...are righteousness and strength" (Isaiah 45:8, 24). Our liturgy has adopted these lines as passionate yearnings for justice and salvation and a Messiah who would bring it. The fulfillment begins in a humble cave where divine love is born in a small baby. Animals breathe warmth. Angel choirs sing about it. Mary and Joseph own almost nothing. God's first appearance is with humble love—no palace, no secure income, no nursery other that what mother nature provides. In adulthood, Jesus said he had nowhere to rest his head. St. Francis of Assisi celebrated Lady Poverty. The history of humble love is God's victory over injustice and sin.

Our Mother Mary, in the ecstasy of her conception of Jesus, sang about the sublime virtue of humility. "He has looked with favor on the lowliness of his servant" (Luke 1:48). A culture drunk with money and pride usually fosters injustice and loss of grace. God's answer is humble love. We tend to use political power and gobs of money to correct abuses of justice. But this only works when we have humble hearts and carry the nonviolent cross. We need soul power far more than cash power. The most durable sign of a saint is humble love, even when the holy one wears a crown such as St. Elizabeth of Hungary.

Holy Mary, Queen of angels and all of us, share with us your devotion to the most powerful form of love—humility.

QUESTION

Why is humble love so strong?

PRAYER

Saving Lord, your example of joyful detachment is inherently appealing. We wonder why we tend to turn away from you and make our usual retreat into self-created plans for our lives. Please give us your vision of humble love to win the battle against injustice.

Thursday of the Third Week of Advent
God Is Always Listening

READINGS

Isaiah 54:1–10   God's anger is momentary. His love is eternal.

Luke 7:24–30   Sinners listened to John the Baptist. The self-righteous did not.

INSPIRATIONAL
QUOTE

On Jordan's bank, the Baptist's cry
Announces that the Lord is nigh;
Awake and hearken, for he brings
Glad tidings of the King of kings.

—Charles Coffin[19]

REFLECTION

No matter how holy we are, we always need some affirmation from God. In spite of all that John knew about Jesus, he sent an odd message to him, "Are you the one who is to come, or are we to wait for another?" (Luke 7:19). From the physical confinement of his prison cell, he ached for affirmation. Severe tests mark the faith journey of anyone, above all for those who have great spiritual gifts such as John the Baptist possessed. The most popular saint of modern times, Mother Teresa, spent many years of her life blessed by God's strong light in her soul, but in her senses there was darkness. With the guidance of her spiritual director she realized that what appeared to be God's divine silence was actually a light that sustained her remarkable ministry. She reached a point where she daily and fervently begged, "Jesus, come be my light."

In our spiritual progress we will all have a stretch of dryness in prayer, when the feeling of God's presence evaporates for a time: "I don't hear God. I think God has left me." In such times we need to recall that despite God's divine silence, he is always listening to us. In the Old Testament history of Israel, the people spent years in exile during which some thought God had abandoned them. Yet those were times of maturing in their faith despite the absence from their temple and the comfort of being in their homeland. Family tragedies, human disappointments, and other forms of suffering are potential growth periods for us. The sparse number of recorded words of Mary in the New Testament may be due to her comfort with divine silence. Faith and silence are twins. Mary knew this.

QUESTION

Is the world too much with me? What are my periods of silence like?

PRAYER

Saving Lord, we know in faith that in you we live and move and have our being. In the times we feel you are far away from us, fill us with the trust that you care for us with your abundant love. With the psalmist we say, "You have changed my mourning into dancing.... I will give you thanks to you forever" (Psalm 30:11, 12).

Friday of the Third Week of Advent
Be a Shining Light of Christ

READINGS

Isaiah 56:1–3a, 6–8	My house shall be called a house of prayer for all people.
John 5:33–36	John was a burning and shining light.

INSPIRATIONAL QUOTE

This little light of mine, I'm going to let it shine.

Everywhere I go, I'm going to let it shine.

On everyone I meet, I'm going to let it shine.

Let it shine, let it shine, let it shine.

—Adapted from "This Little Light of Mine"[20]

REFLECTION

In his Sermon on the Mount, Jesus said to his thousands of listeners, "You are the light of the world" (Matthew 5:14). Addressed to us just as to them, Jesus means we need to become who we are. He uses a folksy example, reminding them they would not light a candle and then hide it under a barrel. People who build cities on hills do so because they want them to be seen. Lawyers know that their witness on the stand must not only be telling the truth—what they say must seem true. The witness must sound like he or she really means it. When speaking about our faith to doubters and scorners, we need to appear as committed believers, to be burning and shining lights of Christ. Say what you mean and mean what you say.

On a cold night it's a good idea to stay near the fire. When our faith cools it's a better idea to stick to the warmth of Christ's presence. One of the reasons for adoration of the Eucharist is that the experience fires up our love for Jesus. Instead of being detached and dull Catholics, we are on fire with Christ. In his great autobiography, *The Seven Storey Mountain,* Thomas Merton recalls how inspiring his visit to Corpus Christi Church in New York was while Benediction was going on. Christ touched him through the obvious faith and reverence of the people from all walks of life. Not only was John the Baptist a burning and shining light of Christ, but Mary drew warmth from the flame year after year from her beloved Son. That's why our nearness to her means we will also be near him.

QUESTION

How do I increase my enthusiasm for Christ?

PRAYER

Lord Jesus, you said to us, "I have come to set the earth on fire and how I wish it were already blazing!" (Luke 12:49). Light our fire, O Lord! If our light doesn't shine, how will others see you? Pope Paul VI taught that the world does not listen to teachers. People listen to witnesses, men and women who shine with burning passion for you, our God. Light our fire!

NOTE: For Saturday of the Third Week of Advent, please refer to the appropriate date on the following pages.

FOURTH SUNDAY OF ADVENT

Nothing Is Impossible With God

READINGS

Isaiah 7:10–14	Behold! A Virgin shall conceive.
Romans 1:1–7	Jesus Christ, descended from David, is the Son of God.
Matthew 1:18–24	An angel tells Joseph that Mary's child comes from the Holy Spirit.

INSPIRATIONAL QUOTE

Where troops of virgins follow the Lamb
Through the streets of the golden city,
Who is she who walks in the lily throng?
The glory of virgins is she, a maiden mother.

—Venantius Fortunatus[21]

REFLECTION

Archbishop Fulton Sheen wrote that there are three ways of generating: carnal, mental, and divine. We are familiar with carnal or sexual generating. We also know that our minds can create new ideas. God sought a way of generating that was neither sexual nor mental, namely, taking a human nature from a virgin and generating a Son while preserving her virginity. If we think this is puzzling, it may reassure us that Mary equally wondered. She asked the angel how this could happen since she had not had relations with a man. Gabriel replied that the Holy Spirit would produce the conception of a child, for nothing will be impossible for God. In our cynical culture many doubt that people can be celibate or virginal, or if they can many think it a waste. Virgin birth seems impossible. But it happened. Mary needed faith to believe it would happen. So do we. She surrendered: "Let it be with me according to your word" (Luke 1:38).

Catholic faith faces many so-called "impossibilities." Jesus is both divine and human. Christ is really present in the Eucharist. He really fed thousands with a few loaves of bread. With a couple of words he drove demons out of a possessed man. He turned gallons of water into wine. He rose from the dead. And so on. Jesus answers our prayers. Sometimes he says no. At other times he astonishes us with a miraculous yes. We want to understand so we can believe. Jesus smiles and tells us we need to believe so we can understand. Our Mother Mary, early on, figured out how to handle it all—she "treasured all these things in her heart" (Luke 2:51). We emphasize our brains. The Bible uses the term heart over one thousand times. It's the secret of faith.

QUESTION

How often do I consult my heart when dealing with faith?

PRAYER

O Lord of Wisdom, you told the two disciples on the road to Emmaus, "O how foolish you are, and how slow of heart to believe all that the prophets have declared!" (Luke 24:25). You could say the same to us. We're better at doubting than believing. We beg you, "overcome our unbelief."

DECEMBER 17

Roots: The Human Ancestors of Jesus

READINGS

Genesis 49:2,   The scepter will not depart from Judah.
8–10

Matthew 1:1–17   The genealogy of Jesus.

INSPIRATIONAL
QUOTE

Lo, how a rose e'er blooming from tender stem
    hath sprung.

Of Jesse's lineage coming as seers of old have sung.

It came a blossom bright amid the cold of winter,

When half spent was the night.

—from "Lo, How a Rose E'er Bloomin"[22]

REFLECTION

Royal families attach great importance to ancestors. Matthew began his Gospel with the ancestors of the King of kings, Christ's family tree. He links Jesus with the royalty of Israel but emphasizes he is our savior. Hebrews were fond of assigning a numerical value to a letter. The letters of King David's name totaled fourteen. Thus the three sets of four-teen names in Christ's genealogy was a method for saying David three times. Matthew connects the beloved King David to the royal child of Bethlehem. If the old David could inspire Israel to dreams of hope, how much more would this thrice-blessed David: Jesus became the universal hope of the world. Luke's Gospel has a genealogy that links Jesus with Adam, whose sin affected us all. Jesus is the new Adam who will redeem us and offer us all his graces.

We Americans are a nation of immigrants who seek identity through looking up our ancestry. We take pride in our famous and successful forebears and blush at the rascals on the family tree. It's a harmless enterprise for the most part, but its value is best seen as a sign of our humanity and dignity. The autobiography of a family may be a story of faith in God or a tale of skepticism and unbelief. Our roots affect our outlooks. So does the current state of family life with its impact on children's faith and life of prayer. The life of Jesus in the Holy Family with Mary and Joseph is a model for our imitation and fulfillment. A daily prayer to that precious family is always a blessing.

QUESTION
What gifts flourish in my family and what shortcomings need healing?

PRAYER
The words of the psalmist about home life could apply most aptly to the home of Jesus, Mary, and Joseph in Nazareth: "How lovely is your dwelling place.... Happy are those who live in your house.... I would rather be a doorkeeper in the house of my God / than live in the tents of wickedness" (Psalm 84:1, 4, 10). While Psalm 84 is actually about the temple, it could have a lot to tell us about the ideal Catholic home. Grace our homes Lord, with this possibility.

December 18
Fling Wide the Portals of Your Heart

READINGS

Jeremiah 23:5–8   God will raise up a righteous descendant to David, namely, the Messiah.

Matthew 1:18–25   Joseph's anxiety about Mary's child is overcome by an angel in a dream.

INSPIRATIONAL QUOTE

Lift up your heads, O mighty gates.

Behold the King of glory waits!

The King of kings is drawing near;

The Savior of the world is here.

—from "Lift Up Your Heads, O Mighty Gates"[23]

REFLECTION

Christmas is a charming story of the birth of a child under difficult circumstances, but it is mellowed by angel choirs, the adoration of the shepherds, and the worship of the Magi. Our manifold decorations, exchanges of gifts, trips to see Santa Claus, the colorful wreaths and lighted trees, the sweet carols that soften the onset of early darkness, the gleam in our children's eyes, make memories that retain a romantic glow from the celebrations. The children's Mass at our packed churches further adds to the magic and the mystery. Behind it all is a call to something permanent, not confined to a few weeks in December. Its welcome beauty is a call to open our hearts to Christ, to make our souls a temple set apart for Christ. Beneath the aroma of the branches of the Christmas tree is an invitation to fall in love again with Jesus.

Seen from Mary's point of view, her trip to Bethlehem was anything but romantic. Her pregnancy is a burden due to her discomfort in riding a donkey for a long trip over hill and dale. She worried about finding a place to stay, winding up in a cave, yet she was comforted by Joseph and deep in faith. It's cold and dark in a strange place. It's lonely without a midwife or family members to help out. Joseph, too, had a husband's concern about all these details. He acted responsibly and faced disappointments. It was all an unlikely setting for the greatest birth in all of history. Then it happened: Christ was born and his infinite beauty made all the rest worthwhile. The distant music of the angels was perfect.

QUESTION

Amid the troubles of giving birth to a child, what are the joys?

PRAYER

God, creator of all life, be with our families in facing the birth of children, caring for them, and raising them in the faith. Grant all families the wisdom needed to be patient and strong in fulfilling this basic calling of all married life.

Come, Divine Messiah. Lead Your People to Freedom

READINGS

Judges 13:2–7, 24–25a

An angel announces the birth of Samson.

Luke 1:5–25

Gabriel announces the birth of John the Baptist to Zachary.

INSPIRATIONAL QUOTE

O Flower of Jesse's stem…kings stand silent in your presence; the nations bow down in worship before you. Come, let nothing keep you from coming to our aid.

—Antiphon for December 19[24]

REFLECTION

As Mary reflected on her extraordinary child to be born, she could remember other evidence of miraculous births such as those of Samson and John the Baptist. She would also know the story of the birth of Hannah's child, Samuel (1 Samuel 1:17–20). Mary's hymn of praise, the Magnificat, echoes Hannah's beautiful hymn at the birth of her son (1 Samuel 2:1–10). The fathers of the Church—marvelous interpreters of Scripture—loved to show how Old Testament events and prophecies were fulfilled in the texts and events of the New Testament. They employed the theme of the history of salvation, a seamless story of God's loving plan to save us. In a particular way they outlined the gradual awareness that a Messiah would come to liberate God's people and the world itself from sin, death, and despair.

Educators like to tell us that expectation affects performance. Teachers who raise the standards for their students generally produce better grades and more enthusiastic cooperation from their pupils. Our Advent walk with Mary keeps before our eyes great expectations for our humanity and spirituality. Our faith tells us that we will not be disappointed. The faith of our fathers and mothers in generations past and the stories of saints, martyrs, and other inspirational people guarantee that our hope is not foolish. Advent expectations, rightly fostered, increase the performance of our spiritual lives. The fervor of our prayer and the intensity of our pursuit of virtue move us joyfully to Christmas.

QUESTION
How would I express what I expect from waiting for Christ?

PRAYER
"You are my hope, O Lord, my trust, O God from my youth. On you we depend from birth." "Upon you I have leaned from my birth; / it was you who took me from my mother's womb /… / I will come praising the mighty deeds of the Lord GOD / … / I still proclaim your wondrous deeds" (Psalm 71:6, 16–17).

DECEMBER 20

And the Word Was Made Flesh and Dwelt Among Us

READINGS

Isaiah 7:10–14   The prophecy of the virgin birth of the Messiah.

Luke 1:26–38   The angel of the Lord declared unto Mary, and she conceived by the Holy Spirit.

INSPIRATIONAL QUOTE

Answer quickly, O Virgin. Reply in haste to the angel…. Answer with a word, receive the Word of God. Speak your own word, conceive the divine Word. Breathe a passing word, embrace the eternal Word.

—St. Bernard[25]

REFLECTION

St. Bernard's vivid sermon, "In Praise of the Virgin Mother," read on December 20 in the Liturgy of the Hours, dramatizes the excitement of the great figures of the Old Testament about Mary's central moment in salvation history. Hear Bernard's words that include his own sentiments: "Tearful Adam with his sorrowing family begs this [a yes] of you…. Abraham begs it, David begs it. All the other holy patriarchs, your ancestors, ask it of you…. Why do you delay?... Let humility be bold, let modesty be confident. This is no time for virginal simplicity to forget prudence…. Open your heart to faith, O blessed Virgin, your lips to praise, your womb to the Creator. See, the desired of all nations is at your door, knocking to enter…. Arise in faith, hasten in devotion, open in praise and thanksgiving."

The urgency of St. Bernard's words has been adopted by the Church in liturgical prayer as a suitable expression of our desire for the coming of Jesus more deeply into our personal lives. His contemplation of one of the most consequential events in the history of salvation visualizes with immense passion this critical moment in the historic conversation between an angel and a very young and sheltered woman in a remote corner of the world. The scriptural text is plain, short, and to the point, with little embellishment, when one thinks of the extraordinary impact of its results. Classical novelists would probe emotions, confusions, options, fears, hopes, and tremblings. St. Luke simply sets it all out before us in twelve verses and we have been contemplating the scene ever since.

Thanks, Mary, for saying "yes" to the angel and "yes" to God.

QUESTION

What challenge does God ask of me these days?

PRAYER

Lord, show us how to follow the example of Mary who was always ready to do your will. You rewarded her faith by making her the temple of your divine Son and the holy ground of his incarnation. Impress on us the tremendous potential that results from obedience to you.

December 21

Blessed Are You for Having Believed

READINGS

Song of Songs
2:8–14

Arise, my beloved, my beautiful one, and come.

Luke 1:39–45

Mary, most blessed are you and blessed is the fruit
of your womb.

INSPIRATIONAL
QUOTE

Elizabeth is the first to hear Mary's voice, but
John is the first to be aware of grace. She hears
with the ears of the body, but he leaps for joy at
the meaning of the mystery…. The women speak
of the grace they have received while the children
are active in secret, unfolding the mystery of love.

—St. Ambrose[26]

REFLECTION

The poem of Trappist monk Thomas Merton, "The Quickening of John
the Baptist," retells the story of Mary's visit to Elizabeth. The moment
Mary greeted Elizabeth, the child leaped in her cousin's womb. Merton
likened Mary's salutation to the sound of a monastery bell, a call to a
faith experience. The unborn John awakens in his mother's womb and

bounds with discovery. It is a dance of faith. What was there about Mary's voice? What secret syllable awoke faith in John? What was it like to be washed in the Spirit of God while yet in the womb? How did he come to know the Jesus cloistered in the womb of Mary? Merton required no words from John. John's movement said it all. It revealed the sheer joy of being filled with God's Spirit. Mary can bring her virgin presence to us as well.

Elizabeth then praised Mary for her faith. "Elizabeth was filled with the Holy Spirit and exclaimed in a loud cry, 'Blessed are you among women, and blessed is the fruit of your womb.... Blessed is she who believed that there would be a fulfillment of what was spoken to her by the Lord'" (Luke 1:41b–42, 45). In our secular culture where belief in God is mocked in movies and on TV and in so-called sophisticated news columns and at the podiums of our universities, would it not be a breath of fresh air to hear Elizabeth's "blessed are you" for believing what your parents taught you, what our Church offered you, what Christ came to foster in you? If we stay near Mary, we will feel a surge of faith in our hearts. Mary is a specialist in the faith department. She knows just how to bring us to faith in Jesus. Ask her.

QUESTION

What areas in my life require growth in faith?

PRAYER

Lord God, you opened the hearts of those lovely couples, Zechariah and Elizabeth, Joseph and Mary, to the wonder of births that beckoned the coming of salvation to our world. Your Spirit moved them to respond with faith. Send us your Spirit to quicken our faith as well.

DECEMBER 22

How Then Should We Sing For God?

READINGS

1 Samuel 1:24–28   Hannah praises God for the birth of Samuel.

Luke 1:46–56   The Almighty has done great things for me.

**INSPIRATIONAL
QUOTE**

My soul magnifies the Lord,
> and my spirit rejoices in God my Savior

for he has looked with favor on the lowliness of
> his servant.

Surely, from now on all generations will call me
> blessed.

—Luke 1:46–48

REFLECTION

Mary's song, the Magnificat, is heard every day in the Church's *Liturgy of the Hours* at Evening Prayer. In thousands of parish rectories, convents, and monasteries—and from a multitude of homes of the laity, Mary's song is heard again. St. Augustine says that if we were asked to sing to please a musician, we would take singing lessons so as not to offend the expert. How then should we sing for God who is the world's most discriminating artist? What words would we pick? Augustine often heard the harvesters of grain and grapes sing while they reaped the crops. After a while they stopped using words. They burst into a jubilant shout. Their cry is beyond words that cannot fully express the joy within their hearts.

This is like the unrestrained roar of happiness at a victory in a game, at the news of the end of a war, at the birth of a child, at the completion of the vows taken at a wedding or an ordination. Mary did indeed use words in her Magnificat, but their tone was radiant joy. This is what God was listening for. This is what the divine music critic wanted to hear. This is exactly what the divine artist did hear from the lips of his beloved Virgin Mary. When we sing for God, we will please his exacting ear by a jubilant cry of joy at reaping such a harvest of love from his affectionate heart. Let us aim at this ideal by believing that, as St. Bede said of Mary, "The Lord has exalted me by a gift so great that language is useless to describe it and the love in my heart can scarcely grasp it."

QUESTION

What will it take for me to offer all the powers of my soul to God?

PRAYER

Loving Lord, you have come to heal the weaknesses in our wills and the stubbornness in our hearts. You came to reconcile us to your creative love and forgiveness. As we plan to celebrate your birth in Bethlehem, help us share more fully in your divine life.

DECEMBER 23

Behold the One Greater Than You

READINGS

Malachi 3:1–4, 23–24   Who will abide the day of the Messiah's coming?

Luke 1:57–66   The birth and naming of John the Baptist.

INSPIRATIONAL QUOTE

Praise to the holiest in the height,
and in the depth be praise;
in all his words most wonderful,
most sure in all his ways.

—Cardinal John Henry Newman[27]

REFLECTION

Alex Haley's memoir, *Roots,* describes the naming story of his ancestor, Kunta Kinte. Eight days after the birth of a child, the father is expected to pick the child's name after much thought and prayer. The unique feature of this custom was that the father kept the name secret until he had whispered it into the ear of his new son or daughter. The family believed the child should be the first one to hear his or her name. After breathing the new name into the child, the father raised the child to the heavens and—saying the name—intoned, "Behold the only one greater than you." This ceremony is similar to what happens at little

John's birth. It takes place eight days after the birth. The father chooses the name. The child is offered to God. Birth is more than a physical event. It is a spiritual moment. The scene evokes what happened when Zechariah named his son John.

Our First Reading today is from the prophet Malachi who anticipates the birth of the Messiah. The text is used by Handel in his grand oratorio, "The Messiah." Those who are familiar with the music can hum the melody here as we cite the words about the world's purification by this wonder child. "Who may abide the day of his coming? And who shall stand when he appeareth? He shall purify the sons of Levi, that they may offer unto the Lord an offering in righteousness" (Malachi 3:2–3, *KJV*). The mysterious event at the home of Elizabeth and Zechariah aroused awe and wonder in their neighbors. They discussed it in their kitchens, at the wells, and in the town square. They concluded, "For, indeed, the hand of the Lord was with him" (Luke 1:66). That would be far truer of the infant born in a cave.

QUESTION

What do I feel when I attend a baptism?

PRAYER

Merciful Father, we use words to communicate our faith in Jesus; stop us from denying him in our deeds. May the gift of your mercy enable us to live chastely, wisely, and prayerfully in our families, friendships, and workplaces. Thank you for the Incarnation.

DECEMBER 24

Rejoice! Rejoice, O Israel! To Thee Shall Come Emmanuel!

READINGS

2 Samuel 7:1–5;   King David will never be forgotten.
8b–12, 27, 29

Luke 1:67–79   The dawn of the Messiah will soon break upon
                   us.

INSPIRATIONAL
QUOTE

O come, the desire of nations, bind
In one the hearts of humankind;
O bid our sad divisions cease,
And be for us our King of Peace.

—Medieval Latin hymn[28]

REFLECTION

Luke introduces the Christmas story on a majestic note of world significance. He asks us to view the birth of Jesus from the throne of the emperor Augustus. The emperor has ordered a census for tax purposes. Mary and Joseph journey to Bethlehem, David's royal city, to be enrolled in the census. Luke links a world ruler to Jesus's birth. The spiritual ruler born in Bethlehem will affect the secular ruler of the known world. A second reason for naming Augustus is that he is the emperor who ended the civil war after Julius Caesar was assassinated. Augustus imposed a *Pax Romana* (Roman peace) on the world. He imposed peace by force. Jesus would initiate peace through freedom, based on love and forgiveness. The greater peace was the *Pax Christi* because it affected the inner self as well as outer society.

Joseph and Mary arrive in a town that showed a heartless lack of hospitality to a pregnant woman. The royal city of David refused a welcome to the newest, greatest, and eternal heir to David's throne. Whenever we fail to show hospitality to anyone, we repeat the coarse sin of the callous people that night. Whenever we fail to welcome Jesus into our own hearts, we play out again the sad story of those who physically turned away Joseph and Mary. In looking back at that holy night, despite all its coldness, both human and seasonal, St. Paul pierces the veil of an indifferent humanity with his words that sound even now trumpetlike: "When the fullness of time had come, God sent his Son, born of a woman…in order to redeem those who were under the law, so that we might receive adoption as children" (Galatians 4:4–5).

QUESTION

How fervent is my calling to hospitality when it is demanded of me?

PRAYER

Lord Jesus, you came into the world to set us free from the forces of evil both within our souls and from the culture in which we live. Set us free to worship you without fear, holy and righteous all the days of our lives.

December 25

Sing, Choirs of Angels

READINGS

Isaiah 9:1–6   A people who walked in darkness have seen a great light.

Titus 2:11–14   The grace of God has appeared to train us to reject godless ways.

Luke 2:1–14   Mary gave birth to the Son of God.

INSPIRATIONAL

QUOTE   Savior, we greet thee, born this happy morning.

Jesus, to thee be all glory giv'n.

Word of the Father, now in flesh appearing.

…

O come, let us adore him, Christ the Lord.

—Latin hymn, eighteenth century[29]

REFLECTION

The birth scene of Jesus is filled with wonderful contrasts. The God whose independence was infinite must look to Mary's milk for survival. The God whose power made the heat of the sun would feel a chill without the swaddling clothes and the warmth of the animals. Infinite power has become vulnerability. Absolute freedom has assumed the annoyances of limits. Our secular culture just sees a human baby. Humanists admire the child. Shepherds and kings adore him. Angels sing his glory. Unbelievers will simply rock the cradle. Believers will let the cradle rock the world. The strong believe power is the ultimate value. The suffering, the poor, and the desperate take heart from their God who comes in such humble surroundings. Already, Jesus knows the human condition and comes to redeem it through sharing in it.

For four weeks we have walked with Mary. Carefully, with faith and prayer, she has led us to the shrine of her Son's birth. From her Immaculate Heart we received the humility we need to empty ours of pride, foolishness, and arrogance. Into this empty space Jesus may enter and change us. The first one to feed him was Mary. She gave him his first meal, mother's milk. Years later he will give us the Lord's Supper, the Eucharist. Mary laid him in a food bin, the manger. Jesus will lie upon an altar, the food bin of eternal life. Mary smiled and welcomed shepherds to adore her little lamb. As Jesus becomes the Lamb of God he gives us shepherds to offer us the sacraments. Mary enjoys hugging her little baby. Her adult Son will thrill to embrace us with love and mercy. The promise in that cave has been fulfilled in Christ's Church and the faith of God's people.

QUESTION

What must I do to receive Jesus with greater faith, hope, and love?

PRAYER

Thank you, Mary, for inviting us to hold Jesus with you. Thank you for the maternal prayers you offered for our intentions. Thank you, Mary, for your song and silences, your humility and care for us. May we kneel with you again and adore your beautiful child.

Final Thoughts on Holding the Child Jesus

Mary has given Jesus the most precious gift that a mother can offer, human life. To walk with Mary is to live again the journey that she experienced in order that the Word could become flesh. Mary reminds us that the magic and the mystery of a newborn baby is the beginning of the adventure of human life. Because this child is also the Son of God, he marvelously enhances human dignity beyond what was ever known before. By comparison this surpasses being born a millionaire, or the child of parents who are famous, powerful, awesome, and influential. The creator of gold is born poor but is immensely rich with the infinity of God. Why else do we recall every Christmas the words of St. Leo the Great: "Christian, recognize your dignity"?

The Magi brought Jesus royal gifts. But their best present was the energy and faith that brought them so many hundreds of miles to find Christ. The shepherds brought Jesus some sheep and lambs to warm the stable. But their best gift was their loving faith and humble gratitude for the greatest event in human history. The angels did what they always do best, sing the melodies of heaven. They wanted the world to know the elegance, beauty, and fervor of this incredible event at Bethlehem.

And now for ourselves. We have already walked with Mary through the Advent days. We feel the surge of faith we hoped for during the journey. We have purchased gifts for family and friends and the poor. We have decorated the tree and framed the front door with lights. If it is winter we have removed snow from the driveway and ice from the steps. Now what are we going to give Jesus? The best answer is the gift of ourselves. How? Give some of your hearts as you look at each other, parents, grandparents, husbands, wives, children, sisters, brothers, cousins, friends, the poor…and yes, those who are a nuisance, who don't much love us, who fail to see how great we all are, and finally, even enemies. Of all the feasts, Christmas is the one that most clearly says, "Give your hearts to others."

Thank you, Virgin Mary, for being our spiritual Mother.

PART TWO

Holding Jesus During His Adult Ministry

The Gospel records of Mary's involvement in Jesus's public ministry are relatively brief. But there is room to link his ministry to his background as a member of the Holy Family and to record his meeting with the religious scholars in the temple when he was twelve—and Mary's reaction. One can also meditate on the "hidden life" of Christ's thirty years in the family home in Nazareth. When Jesus embarks on his preaching life, he often hears praise for his Mother, but he also points out that anyone who hears his teaching and practices is in that sense his mother and brother.

The Cana story brings Mary to the forefront again when she talks to Jesus about the lack of wine for the wedding. Their dialogue transcends the problem when Jesus speaks about his "hour" that is not yet there. Still, Mary tends to the needs of the couple with words that have resonance today: "Do whatever he tells you." This is the last quote from Mary in the Bible.

I draw links in these reflections between Jesus and Mary regarding his miracles, so many of which were works of compassion, a healing sense that was uppermost in their family.

Then I note that Mary would, like typical Jewish mothers of the time, be a storyteller. Jesus carried that to an art form with his parables.

Lastly, I draw attention to Mary's contemplative prayer, which every day held Jesus up and inspired his listeners to come to faith in him. Mary's prayer continues to draw us to Jesus.

Family Life at Nazareth

READINGS

Isaiah 52:7–10   All the world will know God's plan of salvation.

Hebrews 1:1–6   Finally God spoke to us through his Son.

John 1:1–5, 9–14   The Word was made flesh…. We have seen his glory.

INSPIRATIONAL
QUOTE

> Nazareth is a kind of school…. Here, everything speaks to us, everything has meaning. Here we learn the importance of spiritual discipline.
>
> —Pope Paul VI[30]

REFLECTION

If we want to reflect on Mary's impact on the ministry of her Son, Jesus, we should begin with their family life. It is easy to forget that Jesus lived at home for thirty years, all of those years with Mary and part of them with Joseph. Mary and Joseph tutored him up to the beginning of his young adulthood. Unlike most of his peers who usually married quite young, Jesus remained celibate, worked as a carpenter, and lived at home. On the feast of the Holy Family, January 5, 1964, Pope Paul VI delivered a memorable homily during his papal visit to Nazareth. He began by saying that he wished he could have been raised in their holy home and have attended the simple yet profound school that it was. He said that he had taken three lessons from his visit. First he said he learned from their silence. The family treasured peace and quiet. Given the unique people in that house, one might say that they were open to the voice of God's wisdom and the value of study and preparation for a true spiritual life. In this same spirit, Pope Paul said, "How wonderful to be close to Mary, learning…the true meaning of life." This will be a great challenge for us who endure noise, information, news, and all kinds of distractions. But we could call for times of silence for prayer, reading, and inner peace.

The pope said the second lesson from Nazareth is that we learn about the real meaning of family life, especially its enduring character and value for society. It is an ideal setting for raising children and there is no comparable substitute. We need to be a community of love and sharing.

The third lesson was the importance of labor that requires discipline and contributes to the sustenance of the family. The dignity of work is part of life. Jesus's foster father was a carpenter and he became one himself. Our response to the pope's meditation is supported by the inspiring words of St. Paul, "Clothe yourselves with love, which binds everything together in perfect harmony. And let the peace of Christ control your hearts…. Whatever you do in word or deed, do everything in the name of the Lord Jesus" (Colossians 3:14–15, 17).

QUESTION

How could I and my family benefit from the lessons that Pope Paul VI drew from the Holy Family?

PRAYER

We pray for blessings on our family and for special graces for each member. Give us the strength to have a spirit of silence in our homes, to strive to be a family in the best sense of the word, and to be industrious in attending to the physical, spiritual, and human needs of our members.

THE MYSTERY OF CHILDREN

READING

Luke 2:41–52   The finding in the temple.

INSPIRATIONAL
QUOTE

Sing of Jesus, son of Mary,
in the home at Nazareth.
Toil and labor cannot weary
Love enduring unto death.
Constant was the love he gave her,
Though he went forth from her side,
Forth to preach and heal and suffer,
Till on Calvary he died.

—Roland F. Richard Palmer[31]

REFLECTION

When Jesus was twelve years old, the age when he officially reached manhood, he was taken with his parents on a pilgrimage to the temple at Jerusalem. At the end of the pilgrimage the women's caravan left first and the men's a little later. When they caught up with the women it was discovered Jesus was not with them. He had lingered at the temple and was involved in a lively discussion on religious topics among other young men and the rabbis. In a broad sense this was a first, small step in his future ministry. The parents returned to Jerusalem to find Jesus engaged with the religious teachers, listening to them, and asking them questions. "All who heard him were astounded at his understanding and his answers" (Luke 2:47). Joseph and Mary were also astonished, but upset at the anxiety he caused them. Then we hear the first recorded words of Jesus Christ, "Did you not know I must be in my Father's house?" Neither of them understood his reply. They would not be the first parents in history to shake their heads in bewilderment at their offspring's behavior and explanations, even offspring as august as Jesus.

Jesus healed their pain and misunderstanding, not by further explanations, but by obediently returning with them to Nazareth. This is the last we hear from him for the next eighteen years until he begins his public ministry. Mary did not forget the experience. She meditated on it over the years in her heart. During the many years of the "hidden life"—those times of quiet—Mary was in daily contact with the incarnate Son of God. Humanly, she treated Jesus as any mother would. In faith she took in the mystery of her Son as it came to her in thousands of daily exchanges. Scripture draws a veil over those years of communion in which the Mother trained her Son and the Son's mystery revealed itself to her. Like any mother she was pleased to see him grow in age and wisdom. Like the greatest believer who ever lived, she enjoyed seeing Jesus grow in favor before God and people. All parents deal with the obvious steps of development in their children. Many also enjoy the mystery of each child as it reveals itself.

QUESTION

How could Mary help me deal with the humanity and mystery of the children in my life?

PRAYER

Jesus, in your family life, you grew in wisdom, age, and grace before God and people. Help us to follow the same path on our journey toward a loving union with you. With your guidance we can live in a family united in respect and love. In meditating on the words of the Gospels, open our hearts as well as our minds to the profound wisdom contained in them.

Our Relationship With Christ

READINGS

Matthew 12:46–50   Your mother and your brothers await you.

Luke 11:27–28   Blessed is the womb that bore you and the breasts that nursed you.

Mark 3:31–35   Who are my mother and brothers?

INSPIRATIONAL
QUOTE   In Christ there is no east or west,

In him no south or north,

But one great family bound by love.

Throughout the whole wide earth.

—John Oxenham[32]

REFLECTION

To the woman who said, "Blessed is the womb that bore you and the breasts that nursed you," Jesus responded, "Blessed are those who hear the word of God and obey it" (see Luke 11:27–28). This was eminently true of Mary. Again, "your mother and brothers are standing outside." "Who is my mother? Who are my brothers? And stretching out his hand toward his disciples, he said, 'Here are my mother and my brothers! Whoever does the will of my father in heaven is my mother, brother and sister'" (see Matthew 12:47–50). Actually, Mary is the one who really heard the Word of God and kept it in a radical manner. We have already noted the faith of Mary, but more needs to be said in the context of these passages. The faith of Mary, deepened by more than thirty years of prayer and personal contact with Jesus, moved her to cooperate with her Son's mysterious and dangerous mission. The Mother had long ago become a disciple of her Son. Her many years of communion with him along with her surrender to God engendered in her a trust in the divine process that unfolded before her eyes.

No one knows what she might have said to the relatives. Most certainly, she realized that only faith made any sense out of what was happening to Jesus as he became a more controversial person. Somehow, the family must come one day to see Jesus with faith and accept the gift of discipleship. Since the Gospels intrude no further into family privacy, the outcome is left to the imagination and the providence of God. On a different issue, our reflections on Mary and her Son's ministry are limited by the relatively brief number of Gospel passages devoted to Mary. The bulk of the Gospels' attention to Mary is contained in the infancy narratives of Matthew 1—2 and Luke 1—2. Her active presence to a wedding couple in the Cana marriage celebration is another obvious highlight along with Mary's links to Christ's miracles and parables. Lastly, a prominent contribution of Mary to Christ's pastoral care is her marvelous prayer life and contemplative approach. Reading Gospel accounts of Mary's relatives and their coolness to Jesus may be a comfort to many of us who find some family members disinterested in Christ, the Church, the sacraments, saints, and other faith matters. We need to soldier on in our journey of faith. That's what Mary did.

QUESTION

How strong am I in living my faith when lacking support from family members?

PRAYER

Jesus, we need your graces to keep us committed to a relationship with you and the Church. Sometimes family members give up on religion and make life hard for us. Blessed Mary, pray for us and for those who have fallen away. You remained strong through it all. Show us the way.

Mary Calls Jesus to Begin His Ministry

READING

John 2:1–12   Christ's wine miracle at Cana.

INSPIRATIONAL
QUOTE

Mary: They have no wine.

Jesus: My hour has not yet come.

Mary: Do whatever Jesus tells you.

          —adapted from the second chapter of John

"The conscious waters saw their God and blushed."

          —Richard Crashaw[33]

REFLECTION

At the wedding at Cana, Mary notices the wine has run out. She tells her Son about the problem and the embarrassment of the couple. On the surface she is asking simply for a favor, an act of charity for the distressed couple. When Jesus seems to refuse by saying, "My hour has not yet come," it clarifies the deeper aspect of Mary's intervention. She is encouraging him to embark on the road to sacrificial love for our salvation, though this does not mean she foresaw the cross or other details of that sacrifice. At the Jordan, the Father called Jesus to begin his public ministry. At Cana, his Mother called him to the "hour," the more serious and troubling aspect of what his ministry would ultimately demand. This explains his enigmatic response to Mary. Jesus knew what she meant. Their communion as Mother and Son assured that outcome. He is not talking about "clock" time, but rather the crucial time for a turning point, what the Greeks call *kairos*. If this were just a matter of solving a trivial problem, Jesus would not call her "woman." Had he called her "mother" that would refer to her physical parentage. By addressing her as "woman," he was elevating her to a maternal role in the history of salvation. She, too, would suffer with her Son for a great cause.

Christ's words to Mary, which seem abrupt and even unfilial to us are in fact a confirmation of her spiritual motherhood. The Christ light had shone on her faith and revealed to her the spiritual destiny that lay before her. The future beckoned her to open her maternal heart to all people. Nor was this a vague and fuzzy invitation. It was specific and concrete. Decisively, Mary goes to the servants and says, "Do whatever he tells you" (John 2:5). There were six big containers. Jesus told the servants to fill them with water, twenty gallons each. The servants took some to the steward. When he tasted the water made wine, he was astonished and remarked that the family had saved the best wine for last. The wine miracle—like the bread miracle that fed five thousand people—became a prophetic sign of the Eucharistic sacrament of bread and wine that would become Christ's Body and Blood. As St. John's Gospel remembers, Jesus on the cross again spoke to his Mother as "woman," both serving as a mother of the faithful but also participating in his pain with faith that it was a reconciling act on behalf of all who accept salvation. These two scenes in John's account vividly illustrate Mary's influence on her Son's ministry in a manner she never would have imagined. It is why her life story has such a profound impact on us.

QUESTION

How have I participated in Christ's ministry in my life?

PRAYER

Loving Jesus, you courageously involved your Mother in your sacrificial love manifested on the cross. We ask for both insight into what that implies for us as well as for the bravery and wisdom we need to carry our crosses along with you.

Believe in Miracles, You May Need One

READINGS

Matthew 9:1–8	The cure of the paralytic.
John 11:1–44	The raising of Lazarus from the grave.

INSPIRATIONAL
QUOTE

Let others call my faith a lie,

Or try to stir up doubt in me:

Look at me now! None can deny

I once was blind and now I see!

—Fred Pratt Green[34]

REFLECTION

All the Gospels report Christ's miracles. Matthew presents the miracles as transparent events that illustrate the victory of Christ's spiritual kingdom over the forces of evil. Matthew sees the miracles of Jesus in terms of what he is doing, but also stresses their personal meaning. He shows how the Good News of the kingdom takes concrete shape in the healing compassion of Jesus. Christ's words are Gospel. So also are his deeds. Miracles are the nonverbal counterpart of preaching. Healings are the body-talk of Christ's mission. Most miracle stories report the faith of the cured. Jesus asks the blind men, "Do you believe I am able to do this?" (Matthew 9:28). They said "yes," and were healed. Yet miracles alone do not engender faith in all the beholders. The crowds were amazed, but the religious leaders were not amused. "By the ruler of the demons he casts out the demons" (Matthew 9:34). The people sensed the presence of God. The officials said it was the devil. The miracle stirs faith if the observer is open to the possibility. It creates disbelief in those who refuse to see what their eyes tell them. That is why John's Gospel views miracles as moments of judgment separating the believers from the doubters.

As a woman of faith, Mary would have been enormously proud of Christ's healing ministry as manifested in the majority of his miracles. The blind see. The lame walk. A woman's blood flow stops. Lepers are cleansed. Demons are expelled. The hungry are fed. A wedding party gets a gift of wine. A dead man walks alive out of a grave. Mary considered that the flood of compassion pouring out from her Son was the best result of the spiritual attitudes she fostered in her home. Faith was a signature standard at her Nazareth house. It is odd that no Gospel passage reports Mary witnessing a miracle. Apparently, she would only hear about them. What is equally interesting is that today the shrines of Mary are fountains of expectations of miracles. In a sense the Gospel miracles of Jesus continue in the holy ground where Mary appears. Yes, we know the number of actual approved miracles is few, but the miracle of renewed faith is remarkable. Millions of people flow to the sacred spaces of Mary where her Son's power is revealed again so magnificently.

The beauty of it all is that such centers seem like Gospels come alive. Many enjoy movies that try to create scenes from the Gospels. None of them compare to the great Marian shrines. Finally, every Mass actually makes present the healing Christ of the Gospels when the words of the mystery sparkle again while Mary smiles, "This is my Body…. Yes, I know."

QUESTION

What is my attitude regarding miracles?

PRAYER

Jesus, we believe. Help our unbelief. All around us, even in our families, there is need of a miracle. Some have lost faith. Others have serious illness. Yet again alcohol and drugs are a problem. We have more than enough to pray for. Give us courage and hope. Thank you.

Mary's Stories of God

READING

Isaiah 6:1–9   Isaiah beholds the Glory of God and hears his
                   mission to speak of God's holiness.

**INSPIRATIONAL
QUOTE**

Here I am Lord. Is it I, Lord?
I have heard You calling in the night.
I will go, Lord, if You lead me.
I will hold Your people in my heart.

—Daniel L. Schutte[35]

REFLECTION

In biblical times most people grew up in a culture of storytelling. Very likely, Mary treasured stories of God from the Old Testament, and in a special way, the rich messianic stories from Isaiah. In her youth she heard Isaiah read in the synagogue. By the time she had given birth to Jesus, she loved Isaiah's lyrical poetry that vividly captured the vision of God that he had during his call to be a prophet. In her time it was common to tell great stories over and over again. She noticed that her Son had an unusual sense of identity with the prophet's description of his profound encounter with the living God: "I saw the Lord sitting on a throne, high and lofty; and the hem of his robe filled the temple.

Seraphs were in attendance above him;... And one called to another and said: 'Holy, holy, holy is the Lord of hosts; the whole earth is full of his glory'" (see Isaiah 6:1–3). As Jesus said when he was twelve, this was his Father's business: to inspire prophets to proclaim a future Messiah. Mary of course would tell other stories, some which had a humorous touch, such as the visit of three heavenly beings, disguised as humans to the house of Abraham. The patriarch had a feast prepared for them. They told him that Sarah would have a child the next year. She over-heard this and laughed, "Now that I am old and withered.... Shall I really bear a child?" (see Genesis 18:1–15). Isaac was born a year later, just as predicted.

Well trained by his Mother to see the value of stories in speaking of God and the mysteries of God's plans for our salvation, Jesus composed many memorable parables. He used down to earth examples to teach the kingdom of God. Such was his story of the tiny mustard seed that grows into a large bush. The kingdom begins small and grows slowly. Every gardener is familiar with the mystery of growth. The delight that comes from watching inner power take shape in leaves, branches, flowers, and fruit communicates life's mysteries. This also happens in the kingdom. Now that some people are baking their own bread, they can appreciate Christ's parable of the yeast (leaven). Watching a little lump of dough gradually expand into a fluffy loaf ready for the oven is a symbol of the hidden growth of the kingdom of God's love, justice, and mercy. One lesson is, "Do not try to hurry the development of the Church." The other lesson is, "Allow with patience the role of inner grace to perform its miracle of expansion."

QUESTION

What role do stories of faith play in my life and in my family?

PRAYER

Divine Master, we love your stories. We hear them year after year and do not tire of them. We are often too anxious to be thrilled by religion, to get an emotional kick. We know we should become the good ground in which your love and forgiveness can take root. Here's the key to our hearts: Open the door and come in.

MARY'S CONTEMPLATIVE PRAYER

READING

Luke 1:46–55;
2:41–51

Mary kept all these things, treasuring them in her heart.

**INSPIRATIONAL
QUOTE**

I want to walk as a child of the light.
I want to follow Jesus.
God sent the stars to give light to the world.
The star of my life is Jesus.

—Kathleen Thomerson[36]

REFLECTION

Virtually all references to Mary in Scripture include something about her prayer. Her Magnificat is one of the Church's most honored prayers. Early on she learned how to deal with Christ's mysteries by reflecting on them in her heart. With the passing years she quieted potential distractions and focused her affections by directing them to God alone. Her longing for God was due to her receptiveness to the gifts of the Holy Spirit who inflamed her inmost soul. The fire of Christ led her forward with glowing love. Her wisdom had reached the depth necessary for her to be prepared to help people accept Christ's mission by the time Jesus was thirty and ready to start his ministry. Except for the Cana story and the Passion narrative there are no reports in the Gospels about Mary accompanying Jesus and his apostles and disciples in the active ministry. Her contribution was more likely to serve as a pillar of fire, a center of contemplative prayer to assist people to come to faith in her Son. Her gift continues in today's Church among the Carmelites, Trappists, Carthusians, and other contemplative communities. These outposts of deep prayer are a treasure for our parishes and missions of all kinds. When we pray, "Mary, seat of wisdom, pray for us," this is what we seek. Every Eucharist embraces contemplative prayer.

Jesus himself pursued contemplative prayer as an essential part of his active mission. By spending full nights in prayer on a mountain or out in a desert, Jesus models for us the balance we need to get off the treadmill to oblivion that our culture has put us on. This will help us silence our anxieties, our passions, and all the fantasies of our imaginations. All of us could comprehend what God wants of us if we took time off to quicken a longing for God, in sighs of prayer and a passionate desire for union with God. The process is a purification. St. Gregory of Nyssa says, "Once purified, you see things others cannot see. When the mists of sin no longer cloud the eye of your soul, you see that blessed vision clearly in the peace and purity of your heart. That vision is nothing else than the holiness, the purity, the simplicity and all other glorious reflections of God's nature through which God himself is seen."[37] God is not asking us to do something that is impossible to human nature. A wise man once said, "God does not command creatures to whom he has not given wings to become birds, nor those whom he assigned to live on land to live in water." With God's loving help we can pray deeply and confidently.

QUESTION

How strong is my devotion to meditative prayer?

PRAYER

Father, you call us to live in the light of your Son. May we seek the prayers of our Blessed Mother Mary. May she lead us to a relationship with Jesus that will be the most rewarding of friendships. May our prayer strengthen all those who serve the cause of Christ in our world.

Final Thoughts on Holding Jesus During His Adult Ministry

Like all mothers who see their sons grow up and finally leave the family nest, Mary needed to experience Jesus moving out and personally meet the people he came to save. In Mary's case the separation was more acute, for Jesus had lived with his Mother for thirty years and now he was away on his mission in life. Many writers characterize those years as his "hidden life" in contrast with his public life as a preacher, healer, and trainer of the apostles. We have seen Mary holding the child Jesus in her arms. Now she holds him spiritually in the sense that she held him up in deep prayer every day. The first sign of Christ's future ministry was his meeting with the temple scholars without informing Mary or Joseph. Mary was upset with him and said so. Jesus said he had "to be about his Father's business," but apparently this was the last time he did this until the formal beginning of his ministry. In Luke's account of the scene, Mary kept this moment and many others in the future in her heart. This was a biblical way of speaking of her contemplative life in which she held these mysterious truths in prayer.

Pope Paul VI's homily for the Feast of the Holy Family provided us with lessons from those hidden years such as silence, the value of hard work, and the example of fruitful family life. As Jesus became well known he would hear people praise his Mother. Jesus used such occasions to honor those who heard the will of God and kept it. Of course Jesus knew that his Mother was the best example of his standard of faith. He was inviting other family members to live by the same ideal. The story of Cana illustrates a special presence of Mary at a wedding in which the wine supply was gone. She tells Jesus, who replies that his hour had not yet come. We don't hear her reply, but her calling a servant with the words, "Do whatever Jesus tells you" (see John 2:5). These were her last words in the Gospels. But her intercession moved her Son to help the newlyweds. The "hour" of which Jesus spoke was the final chapter of his mission—his Passion and Death. Jesus had called her "woman," not with lack of respect, but honor for her participation in his saving work.

In our discussion of Christ's miracles we suggest that Mary believed these were partly the result of a family life that instilled compassion for those in need: the hungry, the blind, the lame, the possessed, and even bringing back to life a teenage girl and Lazarus, a family friend. In the family life of those years the custom of storytelling was taken for granted. This was a tradition of the Jewish people. Christ's parables were a natural outcome of his own upbringing.

Even today we admire a story that realistically illustrates the truth of life. Certain parables of Christ hit a sympathetic chord in virtually every heart. The story of the Prodigal Son has led us to understand the power and challenge of forgiveness in our lives. That is why many a homily uses the tale to describe God the Father's constant desire to be merciful. Jesus forgave sins during his ministry, right up to his last moments on the cross when he forgives those who were mocking and taunting him. Forgiveness of sins was the very point of his life, death, and resurrection.

While there are few appearances of Mary connected with Christ's public life, there is the fact of her faith and prayer on behalf of Christ's saving work. We may picture her at prayer every day for blessings on her Son. In a way her contemplative prayer was the perfect supplement to Christ's active mission. Our Church has long upheld contemplation in the Latin axiom, *contemplata tradere*, which links contemplative prayer to energizing those in active mission.

Our Church has fostered this valued prayer in religious communities such as those of the Carmelite nuns, the Trappists, and Carthusians. St. Paul says, "Pray always." Thousands have heeded that call and we are blessed by their faith, hope, and love.

Mary, help us to pray with fervor and sincerity every day.

| • PART THREE • |

Holding Jesus During His Passion, Death, Resurrection, and Sending of the Holy Spirit

On the last day of Jesus's life, Mary joins him on the way of the cross and goes directly to Calvary where she gives the example of sharing her Son's grief and lifts him up to the Father. Who can forget Mary holding her Son's body in her arms when he was taken off the cross?

Michelangelo's *Pieta* ("Pity") is arguably the greatest marble evocation of this scene that witnessed the history of salvation. I wonder about the Gospel silence concerning Mary's awareness of the resurrection of Jesus, but I think I hear her singing "Alleluia."

Next, Mary makes her final appearance in the Upper Room where she joins the apostles and disciples in a novena to pray for the coming of the Holy Spirit. In this sense Mary is seen as the Mother of the Church.

As Mary would hold her Son in life and in death and in his ministry, she has the joy of doing the same for us. That is why we are so fond of her.

MARY WALKS THE WAY OF THE CROSS WITH JESUS

READINGS

Matthew 27:27–32   The crowning with thorns and the way of the cross.

Luke 23:26–32   The march to the cross. Jesus meets the faithful women.

INSPIRATIONAL QUOTE

Come, all you who pass by the way,
     look and see
Whether there is any suffering like my suffering,
     which has been dealt me.

—Lamentations 1:12, *NAB*

REFLECTION

The Persians invented crucifixion. The Romans adopted it for the execution of non-Roman criminals, especially murderers and robbers. A trumpeter led Christ's crucifixion procession to the execution mound. The sharp blast of the trumpet both drew a crowd and admonished people to get out of the way of the march. Behind the trumpeter came a herald who carried a wooden poster bearing the name of the criminal and the nature of his crime. This allowed the possibility, according to ancient custom, of having a second trial right on the spot. Someone could produce new evidence and request a new trial. An official from the court would oversee the hearing. If the new evidence proved the prisoner innocent, he would be released. If not, the prisoner, carrying the T-bar of the cross, again walked behind the herald toward execution. The vertical post stood at the mound of execution. Normally four guards marched with the prisoner. A centurion, usually mounted on a horse, came last.

In the popular Catholic devotion, the Stations of the Cross that imagine what Christ's path to Calvary would be like, the fourth station is titled, "Jesus Meets His Mother." Luke's account of the event remembers that Jesus meets a group of women who remained faithful to him. Among them would be Mary who was walking with Jesus. John's Gospel (19:25–27) reports that Mary was present at Calvary. Mothers have long memories, and Mary could recall a prophecy she heard from an elderly holy man, named Simeon, who was present at the presentation of Jesus in the temple. He cradled Jesus in his arms and swayed as he composed a hymn of praise for the Messiah. Then he turned to Mary and predicted that a sword would pierce her heart due to a tragedy that would befall her Son. Now on that hot, dusty afternoon in Jerusalem, Mary realized the truth of Simeon's prophecy. Only the greatest poets can find words to express the mutual pain exchanged in silence between Mother and Son. Instead of words, we are invited to gaze quietly on the scene and let the Spirit touch our hearts. One thing we can say is that Our Lady of Mercy is engaging her beloved Son of Mercy. From the cross, Christ's first words will be, "Father, forgive them, for they know not what they do." This was the final act of Christ's public ministry and Mary was there to share it with him. In faith we can do it too.

QUESTION

What do I feel when I behold the union of Mary and Jesus in the Passion?

PRAYER

Mother Mary, help us resist any temptations of our sinful nature.

Stand With Mary at the Cross

READING

John 19:17–30   The crucifixion and death of Jesus.

INSPIRATIONAL
QUOTE

Strength and protection may thy passion be.

O blessed Jesus, hear and answer me.

Deep in thy wounds, Lord, hide and shelter me,

so I shall never, never part from thee.

—*Anima Christi*, fourteenth-century hymn[38]

REFLECTION

At Cana, Mary had to do what every mother must, let her son go off to his chosen career. At the cross Mary is challenged to let her Son go in a way she would never have imagined. No mother wants to let her son die. No good mother is anxious to release her child to death. When the knife of the Roman soldier pierced the side of Jesus, Mary felt it plunging into her own heart as well. When Jesus committed her to John's care, she knew he was saying, "It's time for you to release me, to let me go into death." Whatever she actually felt remains private. The communion between her and Jesus rests in impenetrable silence. We may correctly conclude she did surrender him to death and let him go. Real love can do no other. Jesus then replied with the word that confirmed the challenge of the cross that he intimated at Cana when he called her "woman" for the first time. She was already the Mother of the Redeemer. In calling her "woman" once more in this situation he confirmed that he wanted her to be the mother of the redeemed. She accepted his dying request to be the spiritual mother of believers. She is always willing to pray for us that our journey to eternal life will be blessed with true fulfillment.

Mary's basic attitude from the day she said "yes" to God at the Annunciation to her "yes" to God again at the cross is the story of her surrender to faith throughout her life. Over and over she prayed, "Let it be done to me according to thy word." Her silence at Calvary gave consent to God's plans for salvation. Rarely has the poetic symmetry of the divine plan been more evident in Scripture. The Catholic tradition of relating to Mary as our spiritual mother originates in this scene at the cross when Jesus commissions her to be mother of the redeemed. "Woman, behold your son." The Catechism confirms this insight into Mary's maternal care: "Mary is clearly the mother of the members of Christ, since she has by her charity joined in bringing about the birth of believers in the Church, who are members of its head" (*CCC*, 963). Centuries of Christian reflection on this call for the spiritual motherhood of Mary has resulted in naming her Mother of Mercy and Seat of Wisdom. These titles enrich our appreciation of Pope Paul VI's teaching when he stated, "We believe that the holy Mother of God, the New Eve,

Mother of the Church, continues in heaven to exercise her maternal role on behalf of the members of Christ" (*CCC*, 975).

QUESTION

How have I experienced Mary's maternal concern?

PRAYER

Heavenly Father, we ask for the intercession of Mary. We ask for her prayers to help us deepen our faith and make progress on the pilgrimage of faith just as she did. We believe that stronger faith will bring us closer to the Church and the many needs of the people we love and serve. We look forward to being closer to Mary and experiencing her maternal care for us.

Mary Receives Christ's Body From the Cross

READINGS

Matthew 27:57–65   The burial of Jesus.

John 19:38–42   The burial of Jesus.

INSPIRATIONAL
QUOTE

In this, your bitter passion,

Good Shepherd, think of me

With your most sweet compassion,

Unworthy though I be.

Beneath your cross abiding,

Forever would I rest,

In your dear love confiding,

And with your presence blessed.

—St. Bernard of Clairvaux[39]

REFLECTION

Christian faith, imagination, and art have often supplemented what Scripture does not say. Such is the case of how Mary received her Son's body when it was removed from the cross. A number of sculptors created various versions of the scene they called *Pieta* or "the Pity." Michelangelo created the greatest and most widely admired *Pieta*. The artist took two years to carve it from marble. To assure its authenticity he persuaded the Grand Rabbi of Rome to permit young Jewish men and women to pose for the hundreds of sketches he made so that Jesus and Mary would have credible Semitic faces. The sculptor imagined a Mary who was finally alone for a time with her deceased Son. Though most paintings and sculptors portrayed crowd scenes, Michelangelo judged that the best approach would show Mary and Jesus alone. There would be no soldiers, no angels, no hangers-on. Since Jesus was dead there would be no emotion in his face to show how he felt for his Mother. The artist presented Mary's face filled with her feelings for her Son.

Never heard from while Jesus was alive, Joseph of Arimathea undertakes the risky business of claiming the body from the Roman governor, and then donating his new tomb in the garden next to Calvary. Ever the cautious conservative during Jesus's life, unwilling to be seen with him publicly, Nicodemus throws caution to the wind and joins Joseph in preparing the burial by purchasing elaborate amounts of aloes and myrrh.

Though Mary was a woman in her early fifties, the sculptor preferred to represent her as a young woman, sensitive and strong enough to hold Jesus in her lap. He was heavy but the burden in her heart was the real weight. The sculptor bathed the two figures in calm and peace. Beauty can reveal the sacred just as well as tormented pain, and at the same time thrill the viewers. A cardinal asked Michelangelo, "Tell me, my son, why does the Madonna's face remain so young—younger than her son's?" He replied, "Your grace, it seemed to me that the Virgin Mary would not age."[40] She was pure and would have kept the freshness of youth. In the sculpture, Jesus rests calmly in Mary's arms; the nail holes in his hands and feet are tiny dots. The *Pieta* is enshrined in St. Peter's Basilica in Rome.

QUESTION

How does Michelangelo's *Pieta* help me to feel close to Mary's sorrow?

PRAYER

We adore you, O Christ, and we praise you, for by your holy cross you have redeemed the world. Mary, with you we stay near Jesus in this calm and awesome scene, and ask that you share with us your capacity to stay so close to Jesus in a spiritual attitude of surrender and peace.

CHRIST IS RISEN, ALLELUIA! HE IS RISEN INDEED, ALLELUIA!

READINGS

Luke 24:1–35   Christ's resurrection and his walk to Emmaus with two disciples.

John 20:1–29; 21:15–19   The empty tomb, appearances to Magdalene, the apostles, Thomas, Peter.

INSPIRATIONAL QUOTE

When our hearts are wintry, grieving, or in pain,
Your touch can call us back to life again.
Fields of our hearts, dead and bare have been
Love is come again, like wheat arising green.

— John M.C. Crum[41]

REFLECTION

In the Ukraine the common Easter greeting is *Christos Voskrese!* and the response is *Voistinu Voskrese!* (Christ is risen! He is risen indeed!) It's like "Merry Christmas" for us. The children grow up in a culture that has found this simple way to spread the Good News of Christ's resurrection from the dead as if once again for the first time. Amazingly, seventy years of Communist oppression never blotted out this testimony to the glorious victory of Jesus over death. The Easter stories in the Gospels are full of drama. Christ's first appearance was to Mary Magdalene whose love kept her near the tomb until she could be satisfied with Christ's revelation. Peter and John hasten to the tomb, John quicker than Peter who simply saw the empty chamber without comment. But John saw and believed. Both came to faith. Slowpoke Peter weaved his way heavily to Christ's heart, while John was like a gifted eagle soaring to the sun. Later, two disciples on the road to Emmaus received a Scripture lesson from the Risen Christ and only recognized him at a meal in town. Their broken hearts were healed by the broken bread of Eucharist. Many of us would like to be John, but the truth is we are closer to snails than eagles. Our faith life is much like Peter's with a persistence that finally reaches Jesus.

The curious silence of the Gospels about Mary and the resurrection is strange, which is probably why some imagine Mary knew about the resurrection before anyone else. We will never know. One thing is sure, Mary soon heard the great news and could well have been at one of the appearances recorded by St. Paul: "Then he appeared to more than five hundred brothers and sisters at one time, most of whom are still alive" (1 Corinthians 15:6). Her lifelong growth in continuing union with God and the blessings that were hers in the divine plan of salvation moved her to praise God with a full heart for the resurrection of her Son. "Raise to him a new psalm; exalt him, and call upon his name / ... / I will sing to my God a new song: / O Lord, you are great and glorious, / wonderful in strength, invincible." (Judith 16:1, 13). What virtue dominates such a full-throated acclamation of God and his Son? Love that awakens faith is the secret. St. Augustine, who loved the music of faith, wrote that God cries out, "Love me and you will have me, for you would be unable to love me if you did not already possess me."[42]

QUESTION

How has Christ's resurrection increased my faith in him?

PRAYER

Christ, our hope, you have arisen. Praise and glory be yours! With your Mother Mary, we greet your resurrection with a burst of new faith in you and a fresh hope for a life that prepares us for eternal life and for a growth in love and service to our families, friends, and anyone in need.

Mother of Jesus, Mother of the Church

Acts 1:13–14;   Mary joins the disciples in the Upper Room to
2:1–41   prepare for the coming of the Holy Spirit.

INSPIRATIONAL

QUOTE   Come Holy Ghost, Creator blest,

And in our hearts take up thy rest.

Come with thy grace and heav'nly aid

To fill the hearts which thou hast made.

—*Veni, Creator Spiritus*[43]

REFLECTION

We reported Mary's intercessory prayer at Cana, now we see Mary in the Upper Room with the disciples of Jesus during the nine-day novena before Pentecost. Her prayer witness is there for all to behold. Mary believed long before the others—at Nazareth, in Bethlehem, in Egypt, at the temple; at Cana, during Jesus's public ministry; and finally, at the cross where she hoped against hope. Her faith did not fail at Calvary. As Abraham became the father of faith for the first covenant, Mary became the mother of faith for the members of the Christian covenant. At Easter the promise she heard at Nazareth rang like cathedral bells in her heart, for all she believed came true. As the Church was being born, its members stood next to Mary, the first believer in Jesus who already had a faith pilgrimage of thirty-three years behind her. As they observed her they would be drawn to affirm what Elizabeth said long ago, "Blessed are you who believed that what was spoken to you would be fulfilled" (see Luke 1:45). They felt the special presence of a woman who was a unique witness to the mystery of Jesus from the moment of his conception.

Our pilgrimage with Mary throughout the meditations in this book reflects seven qualities of the faith of Mary: personal, graced, free, convinced, communal, focused, and involved in the cross. It should comfort and inspire us to know that Mary realizes what we face on our own faith journeys. She walks in union with you and me and the whole Church. Like those at Pentecost we can see her through Jesus and see Jesus through her. We should let no day pass without getting closer to Mary. She knows our needs, and her maternal heart wants to love and care for us. Like the moon that points gratefully to the sun for its light, Mary's purpose is to point us to Jesus and the Church and the needs of others. In the Upper Room at Pentecost the Church looked at Mary through the window of Jesus. Today the Church looks at Jesus through the translucent witness of Mary. At the descent of the Holy Spirit, Mary is not apart from the Church but in its very midst in communion with the members. She holds a special place among them for she is like a mirror in which is reflected the wonders of God. St. Bernard thought of

Mary as a star leading us to Christ. He said, "See that star, call on Mary." Good advice, don't you think?

QUESTION

How much closer have I come to Mary as a result of this little book?

PRAYER

Loving Father, may the prayers of the Virgin Mary bring us closer to Christ and the Church. Through her intercession may we participate in the sacraments more actively and dedicate ourselves to witness Christ's kingdom of love, justice, and mercy. Thank you, God, for giving us Mary as our spiritual mother.

Final Thoughts on Holding Jesus During His Passion, Death, Resurrection, and Sending of the Holy Spirit

Having reviewed Mary's role in Christ's public ministry, we then meditated on her participation in the passion and death of Jesus. True love never abandons the beloved who is facing unjust treatment, cruel beatings, humiliation from the palace guard, and the ghastly punishment of being nailed to a cross. Mary walked with Jesus to Calvary. She stood by him on his bed of pain. She heard him say to John, "Son, behold, your mother." Centuries of popular devotion has seen in Christ's commission of Mary to consider John as a son, a call to her maternal care for the Church's members.

She held him in her arms immediately after his death. We can remember her holding the baby Jesus in her arms at Bethlehem. We cannot forget her resting the dead body of her Son in her arms. Films of that scene usually portray her as wailing in her grief. I suggest that she who cultivated the productive habit of silence would have gazed in quiet dignity at him, as Michelangelo's *Pieta* conveyed so well. The visceral witnesses were on display. Mary countered that with her silent dignity and love. One thing she learned better than most of us is that in such a violent killing of her Son, his life is changed, but not taken away.

The Sunday morning news about Christ's Resurrection was conveyed to her. Christ had risen from the dead. It's odd that there is no Gospel report of the Risen Jesus appearing to his Mother. Popular devotion tends to create scenes depicting the Risen Christ appearing to Mary. Sacred history has drawn a curtain over Mary's participation in the Resurrection and how it may have occurred and has not speculated about it. Mary's story then brings us to the Upper Room where 120 disciples were gathered in prayer for the coming of the Holy Spirit. Mary was there, praying with the others for the coming of the Spirit. Most paintings and icons picture of the Pentecost event show Mary sitting in the midst of the apostles in the place of honor. Mary was familiar with the creative powers of the Holy Spirit, having experienced them at the Annunciation when she asked how she could have a child without being married. The angel Gabriel said, "The Holy Spirit will come upon you and the power of the most high will overshadow you" (see Luke 2:35). And so the Word became flesh and dwelt among us.

We now conclude our reflections on Mary. I have asked you take an Advent walk with Mary as she prepares to give birth to Jesus. I also asked you to meditate on Mary's involvement in her Son's public ministry. Lastly, I invited you to participate in Mary's Stations of the Cross with Jesus as she stood with him until his battered body was lowered into her arms. Three days later Mary would sing an alleluia for the Resurrection of Jesus. Finally, we saw Mary seated in the chair of honor during the novena prayed for the coming of the Holy Spirit. Her maternal interests now include the Body of Christ.

Mary does not ask us to concentrate on her. She called herself the handmaid of the Lord. The handmaid's eyes are not on herself, but on her Lord. Mary is a mirror of Christ and the Church. She says, "When you look at me in faith, you will see your Savior, Jesus Christ, and the Church which is the sacrament of salvation. I will gently turn your attention to your goal and destiny in God. I am your spiritual mother who will listen to your needs and bring them to my Son. I am not self-absorbed. I will help you to transcend yourself, so you can find true personal fulfillment. Because I love you with a mother's love, I will do this for you. I can do this because my Son makes it possible for me to assist you. Yes, I love you."

Ave Maria.

1. Available at http://cantusmundi.blogspot.com/.

2. Hymn from the *Baltimore Catechism*, available at http://campus.udayton.edu/mary/resources/music/balthymns.html.

3. Quoted in Enzo Lodi, *Saints of the Roman Calendar: Including Feasts Proper to the English-Speaking World* (New York: Society of St. Paul, 1992), p. 145.

4. Pope Paul VI, *Marialis Cultus*, quoted in Alfred McBride, *Images of Mary* (Cincinnati: St. Anthony Messenger Press, 1999), p. 4.

5. St. Bernard of Clairvaux, Hom. II, "Super Missus est," 17; Migne, P.L., CLXXXIII, 70-b, c, d, 71-a.

6. See Psalm 131:2 or the *Liturgy of the Hours* (New York: Catholic Book, 1988), vol. I, p. 972.

7. Alexander Pope, "The Universal Prayer." Available at www.poetryfoundation.org/poem/180945.

8. Hymn by Bianco da Siena, translated by Richard F. Littledale. Available at http://www.oremus.org/hymnal/c/c186.html.

9. Quoted in *Liturgy of the Hours*, Hymns for the Advent Season, vol. 1, p. 124.

10. Quoted in *Liturgy of the Hours*, vol. I, p. 1229.

11. *Liturgy of the Hours*, vol. I, p. 1231.

12. Christina Rossetti, "In the Bleak Midwinter." Available at www.poetryfoundation.org/poem/238450.

13. Quoted in *Liturgy of the Hours*, Office of Readings, vol. I, p. 184.

14. "Once in Royal David's City." Available at http://www.carols.org.uk/once_in_royal_davids_city.htm.

15. *Liturgy of the Hours*, vol. I, p. 386.

16. "We Three Kings of Orient Are," available at http://www.carols.org.uk/we_three_kings_of_orient_are.htm.

17. Quoted in *Liturgy of the Hours*, vol. I, Office of Readings, p. 1267.

18. Words of Father Zossima in Dostoevsky's *The Brothers Kramazov*. Available at www.whoislikegodmichael.tumblr.com/post/8804275664/at-some-thoughts-a-man-stands-perplexed-above.

19. "On Jordan's Bank," translated by John Chandler. Available at http://www.cyberhymnal.org/htm/o/n/onjordan.htm.

20. Traditional Gospel hymn. Available at www. gospel-music.de/Gospel-Lyrics.html.

21. Translated by Sister Maura, quoted in McBride, *Images of Mary*, p. 21.

22. *"Es ist ein Ros entsprungen," Speier Gebetbuch*, 1599. Translated by Theodore Baker. Available at http://openhymnal.org/Lyrics/Lo_How_A_Rose_Eer_Blooming-Es_Ist_Ein_Ros_Entsprungen.html.

23. George Weisel, translated by Catherine Winkworth. Available at http://www.hymnsite.com/lyrics/umh213.sht.

24. *Liturgy of the Hours*, vol. I, p. 342.

25. Second Reading for December 20, *Liturgy of the Hours*, vol. I, p. 345.

26. Office of Readings for December 21, *Liturgy of the Hours*, vol. I, pp. 353–354.

27. Quoted in "The Dream of Gerontius," *The Month: An Illustrated Magazine of Literature*, Science and Art, 1865.

28. Translated by John M. Neale. Available at http://www.oremus.org/hymnal/o/o084.html.

29. Translated by Frederick Oakley, Hymn for the Christmas Season, from *Liturgy of the Hours*, vol. I, p. 388.

30. Quoted in *Liturgy of the Hours*, vol. I, pp. 426–427.

31. "Sing of Mary, Pure and Lowly," available at http://www.catholicdoors.com/songs/marian/maria011.htm.

32. William A. Dunkerly/John Oxenham, "In Christ There Is No East or West." Available at http://www.cyberhymnal.org/htm/i/c/iceaswes.htm.

33. Quoted by Fulton Sheen at www.fultonsheen.com/Fulton-Sheen-articles/Calvary-and-the-Mass---II.cfm?artid=35.

34. "He Healed the Darkness of My Mind," available at http://www.hymnary.org/hymn/GATHER/876.

35. "Here I Am, Lord," available at www.godtouches.org/cathhymns.html.

36. From "I Want to Walk as a Child of the Light," available at http://cantus-mundi.blogspot.com/2010/07/i-want-to-walk-as-child-of-light.html.

37. Quoted in the *Liturgy of the Hours*, vol. III, p. 414.

38. From "Soul of My Savior," available at www.chantcd.com/lyrics/soul_of_my_savior.htm.

39. From "O Sacred Head Surrounded," translated by Henry Baker. Available at http://www.oremus.org/hymnal/o/o541.html.

40. These details of Michelangelo's *Pieta* have been adapted from Irving Stone's vivid novel based on the life of this great artist, *The Agony and the Ecstasy* (New York: Doubleday, 1961), pp. 338–359.

41. From "Now the Green Blade Rises," available at http://www.missionstclare.com/music/pascha/green_blade/238c.html.

42. Augustine, Sermon 34.

43. From "Come, Holy Ghost," text attributed to Rabanus Maurus, translated by Edward Caswall. Available at http://www.ourladyswarriors.org/indulge/g61.htm.

About the Author

ALFRED MCBRIDE, O.PRAEM., holds a diploma in catechetics from Lumen Vitae, Brussels, and a doctorate in religious education from the Catholic University of America. He is the author of *A Priest Forever: Nine Signs of Renewal and Hope; The Story of the Church;* and *A Short History of the Mass.*